DINOSAURS

by Dougal Dixon

BACKPACKBOOKS
○
NEW YORK

For coedition titles: This edition 2004 Backpack Books by arrangement with ticktock Media Ltd.
Backpack Books
122 Fifth Avenue
New York, NY 10011

Printed in Taiwan

10 9 8 7 6 5 4 3 2 1

C O N T E N T S

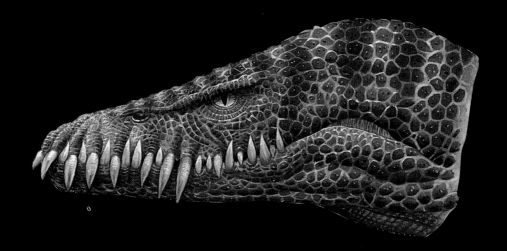

Carnivores	4	The first swimmers	68
Where did they come from?	6	A school of swimming reptiles	70
The first known	8	Placodonts – the shell seekers	72
Early hunters	10	Between the land & the sea	74
Crest-headed beasts	12	The giants of the sea	76
Spinosaurids – the fish eaters	14	A range of pliosaurs	78
The smallest dinosaurs	16	Elasmosaurs – the long necks	80
Jurassic giant	18	Elasmosaur lifestyle	82
Fast hunters	20	Ichthyosaurs – the fish lizards	84
Eggs & nests	22	A range of ichthyosaurs	86
Bird or dinosaur?	24	Ichthyosaurs – dispelling a myth	88
Bird mimics	26	Mosasaurs	90
Segnosaurids	28	Crocodiles	92
Tyrannosaurids	30	**In the Sky**	94
The new kings	32	The pioneers	96
Herbivores	34	Early flying reptiles	98
The first plant-eating dinosaurs	36	The discovery of the pterosaurs	100
Life of the prosauropods	38	The earliest pterosaur	102
Sauropods	40	Big heads	104
The heyday of the sauropods	42	Soft coverings	106
The last of the sauropods	44	The most famous	108
Ornithopods — the bird feet	46	Heads & crests	110
The *Iguanodon* dynasty	48	The biggest	112
The duckbills	50	The first bird	114
The plated lizards	52	Chinese "Gang of Three"	116
A world of stegosaurs	54	Toward modern birds	118
The nodosaurids — spiky dinosaurs	56	Abandoning flight	120
Ankylosaurids — the club-tails	58	Since the dinosaurs	122
Boneheads	60	Did you know?	124
The primitive-horned dinosaurs	62	Glossary	125
The big-horned dinosaurs	64	Index	126
In the Sea	66	Acknowlegements	128

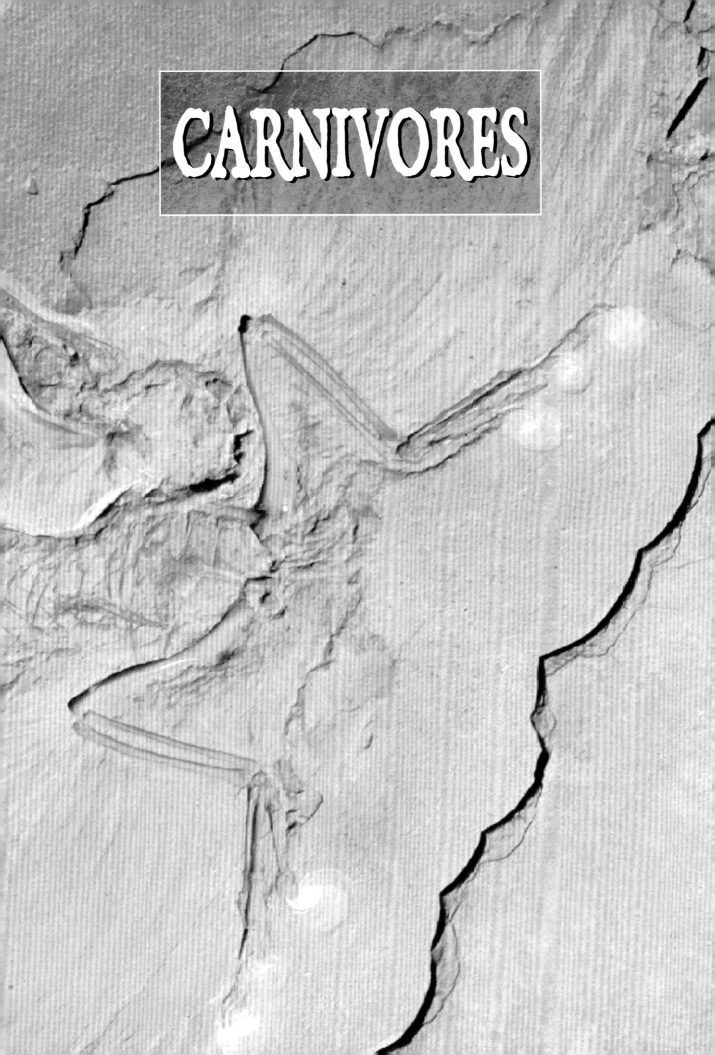

CARNIVORES

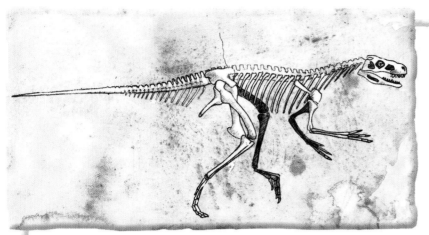

POWERFUL LEGS

Herrerasaurus, a meat-eating dinosaur, walked on strong hind legs with its teeth and the claws on its arms held out in front, where they could do the most damage. *Herrerasaurus*'s back was held horizontally, and the body was balanced by a long tail. This structure became the pattern for all meat-eating dinosaurs.

BEFORE THE DINOSAURS

During the Permian Period, the main plant-eating animals of the time were mammal-like reptiles. They had teeth like mammals, and some were even hairy. The biggest, such as the broad-headed *Moschops*, shown here, were built like hippopotami. At about the same time as the first dinosaurs evolved, the first mammals evolved, too. Descended from the mammal-like reptiles, they were small and furry and bore live young. If the dinosaurs had not come to prominence, the mammals might have taken over. Instead, they had to wait 160 million years before evolving into more successful species.

EORAPTOR

Eoraptor was about the size of a fox and, like all the dinosaurs to follow, walked on legs that were held straight under its body. This structure made it a much faster animal than the other reptiles that walked on legs sprawled out to the side.

TIGER-SIZED

Herrerasaurus was about the size of a tiger and thus was a much bigger animal than *Eoraptor*. One of the first dinosaurs, it was a primitive theropod, part of the group that includes all the meat eaters. Adults could reach a length of 10 feet (3 m). The skeleton of a *Herrerasaurus* was found in Argentina, in South America.

WHERE DID THEY COME FROM?

Dinosaurs! The most famous of all extinct animals, these reptiles, most of them whale-sized, dominated Earth for about 160 million years. Reptiles evolved during the Carboniferous Period, about 350 million years ago, and flourished in the succeeding Permian, Triassic, Jurassic, and Cretaceous periods. During this time, there were land-living reptiles, swimming reptiles, flying reptiles, herbivores (plant eaters), carnivores (meat eaters), and omnivores (both plant and meat eaters) — reptiles of all kinds in every environment. The age of reptiles was well under way before the first dinosaurs appeared around the end of the Triassic Period, about 225 million years ago. At the end of the Cretaceous Period, about 65 million years ago, all the big reptiles died out, and mammals took over.

EORAPTOR SKULL

An x-ray photograph of *Eoraptor's* skull shows how its lightweight skull was made up of thin struts of bone. The dinosaur's light bone structure enabled it to move fast. The skulls of most subsequent meat-eating dinosaurs were built like this.

RAUISUCHIAN

Before the dinosaurs came along, the biggest of the hunters was a group of land-living crocodile relatives called rauisuchians. They had big heads and many sharp teeth, and, although they were slow-moving, they were faster than the plant-eating reptiles that abounded at the time.

CARBONIFEROUS 354-290 MYA	PERMIAN 290-248 MYA	TRIASSIC 248-206 MYA	EARLY/MID JURASSIC 206-159 MYA	LATE JURASSIC 159-144 MYA

LIKE MEGALOSAURUS?

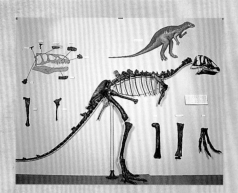

For a long time, the name *Megalosaurus* was applied to the fossil of any meat-eating dinosaur found in Britain or Europe. All kinds of unrelated dinosaurs were erroneously given the name. Only now is this mixture of different animals being sorted out. One of the dinosaurs once thought to be a *Megalosaurus* is a virtually complete skeleton of *Eustreptospondylus* in the Oxford University Museum in England.

MEGALOSAURUS JAW

The lower jawbone and teeth of *Megalosaurus* were the first parts of the animal to be discovered. They were found in Oxfordshire, England, in about 1815. The Reverend William Buckland studied them and deduced from the sharp, pointed teeth that they had belonged to a meat-eating animal and that it had been a large reptile. Other scientists studied the remains in the 1820s and one of them — history does not tell us who — came up with the name *Megalosaurus*.

FIRST DINOSAUR THEME PARK

Because of the great public interest in science in the mid-19th century, part of Crystal Palace park in South London was developed as an ancient landscape. Statues (which still stand today) were erected showing the three dinosaurs and the marine reptiles that were known at the time. All that was known of *Megalosaurus* was its jawbone, teeth, and a few fragments of bone. Since nobody knew what the animal actually looked like, it was modeled as a fearsome, four-footed, dragonlike creature.

TRIASSIC 248-206 MYA	EARLY/MID JURASSIC 206-159 MYA	LATE JURASSIC 159-144 MYA	EARLY CRETACEOUS 144-97 MYA	LATE CRETACEOUS 97-65 MYA

THE FIRST KNOWN

Since civilization began, people have known about giant bones embedded in rocks. In earliest times they were spoken of in legends as the bones of giants and dragons and other mythical creatures. By the early 19th century, however, scientific knowledge had advanced sufficiently for scientists to appreciate the true nature of fossils. In 1842, the British anatomist, Sir Richard Owen, invented the term "dinosauria" (terrible lizards) to classify three fossil animals whose skeletons had been discovered in England during the previous two decades. One was the plant-eating *Iguanodon*, which is now quite well known. Another was the armored *Hylaeosaurus*, which we still know very little about. The first of the trio to be brought to light and described was the carnivorous *Megalosaurus*.

WILLIAM BUCKLAND (1784–1856)

This 19th-century clergyman was typical of his time. When not in the pulpit, he spent his extensive spare time doing scientific research. Most of the fossils he studied were of sea-living animals — seashells and marine reptiles. Fossils of land-living animals have always been more rare (*see page 124*). He may not have invented the name *Megalosaurus*, but he was the scholar who did all the scientific work on it.

MODERN VIEW

Even today, we do not have a clear idea of what *Megalosaurus* looked like because so few fossilized remains have been found. Like all meat-eating dinosaurs, it must have walked on its hind legs with its big head held well forward, balanced by a heavy tail. Fossils found in lagoon deposits in what is now Normandy in northern France suggest that *Megalosaurus* was a shoreline scavenger that prowled the beach, eating dead things that had been washed up.

EARLY HUNTERS

Most early meat-eating dinosaurs were small, some no bigger than our cats and dogs. They probably fed mainly on even smaller animals, such as lizards and early mammals. However, most plant-eating reptiles of the time were large animals and would also have made good prey for meat eaters. Some of the early dinosaurs adopted a strategy of hunting in packs so they could bring down and kill some of these big plant eaters. Today, such teamwork is still used in the wild by animals such as Canadian wolves, which hunt moose bigger than themselves. Similarly, on the African plains, groups of hyenas attack wildebeest that are far bigger than they are.

THE CONNECTICUT FOOTPRINTS

At the beginning of the 19th century, long before anybody knew anything about dinosaurs, farmers in New England kept finding three-toed trackways in Triassic sandstone at the foot of the Appalachian Mountains, shown above. At first it was believed the footprints were made by giant birds that existed in the area before Noah's flood, as described in the Bible. We now know they were footprints of dinosaur packs, probably made by *Coelophysis* or something that resembled *Coelophysis*.

TRIASSIC	EARLY/MID JURASSIC	LATE JURASSIC	EARLY CRETACEOUS	LATE CRETACEOUS
248-206 MYA	206-159 MYA	159-144 MYA	144-97 MYA	97-65 MYA

BIRD & DINOSAUR FOOTPRINTS

Birds and dinosaurs are so closely related it is little wonder the footprints of one could be mistaken for those of the other. In a series of ridges of Jurassic and Cretaceous rocks in the flanks of the Rocky Mountains west of Denver, there are fossilized footprints of both dinosaurs and birds. Bird footprints can be distinguished from dinosaur prints by the greater spread of their toes — about 90° as opposed to about 45°. There is also often a trace of the little fourth toe pointing backward. In dinosaurs, this toe is usually well clear of the ground.

DINOSAUR

BIRD

ONE WORLD

In Late Triassic and Early Jurassic times, Earth was very different from the way it is today. All the continental landmasses were joined together in one area, called Pangaea. Since there was only one landmass, animals of the same kind were able to migrate everywhere. This is why we find the remains of almost identical animals in New Mexico and in Connecticut, as well as in Zimbabwe, thousands of miles away on the African continent.

SYNTARSUS

In 1972, a remarkable deposit of fossils was found in Rhodesia (now Zimbabwe). A mass of bones lay in fine river sediment, sandwiched between rocks formed from sand dunes. The fossils were of a pack of small, meat-eating dinosaurs of different sizes and ages. They seemed to have drowned in a flash flood that struck as they were crossing a dry river bed. These meat-eating dinosaurs, named *Syntarsus*, were almost identical in build to *Coelophysis*, and some scientists believe they were a species of the same animal.

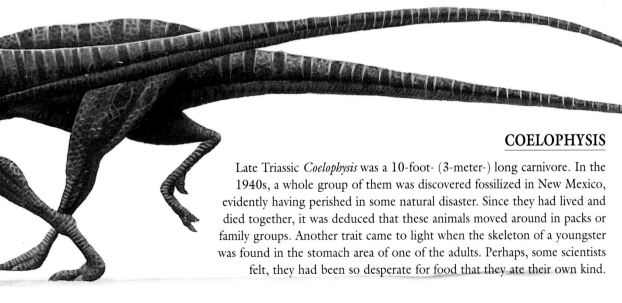

COELOPHYSIS

Late Triassic *Coelophysis* was a 10-foot- (3-meter-) long carnivore. In the 1940s, a whole group of them was discovered fossilized in New Mexico, evidently having perished in some natural disaster. Since they had lived and died together, it was deduced that these animals moved around in packs or family groups. Another trait came to light when the skeleton of a youngster was found in the stomach area of one of the adults. Perhaps, some scientists felt, they had been so desperate for food that they ate their own kind.

CREST-HEADED BEASTS

Look at the bright colors of many birds — the long tail feathers of a peacock, the gaudy bill of a toucan, the red breast of a robin. Color is part of a bird's method of communication. A bird's brain can "read" the colors it sees, enabling the bird to recognize whether another bird is a friend or foe. Birds are related to dinosaurs (*see pages 24–25*), which had similar brains and senses. It is very likely that dinosaurs also used color for communication. Some dinosaurs (especially among the carnivores) had crests and horns as brightly colored as the plumage of modern birds.

DILOPHOSAURUS IN LIFE

When it was alive, *Dilophosaurus* probably looked dazzling. Its crests may have been particularly colorful to frighten rivals or attract a mate from far away. The rest of the animal, including its dewlaps (flaps of skin beneath the chin), may also have been brightly colored to back up the signals given by the crests.

FORWARD THINKING

The Early Jurassic meat eater from Antarctica, *Cryolophosaurus*, had a crest that curled up and forward above its eyes. The bony core was probably covered with brightly colored horn or skin. *Cryolophosaurus* is the only dinosaur known to have had a crest that ran across the skull, from side to side, rather than along it, from front to back. At 26 feet (8 m) long, it was probably the biggest meat eater of its time, its size enhanced by the crest.

HORNED MONSTER

In the Late Jurassic, one of the fiercest dinosaurs, *Ceratosaurus*, lived in North America and Tanzania. It had a heavy head with a horn on the nose and two horns above the eyes. The heavy skull suggests they may have fought by head butting, but the horns were lightly built and would not have been much use as weapons.

MONOLOPHOSAURUS

The crest of *Monolophosaurus*, a medium-sized, Middle Jurassic, meat-eating dinosaur from China, was made up of a pair of skull bones fused together and growing upward. Air gaps and channels between the bones were connected to the nostrils and may have amplified grunts and roars generated in the animal's throat. In this way the crest would have helped it communicate.

DILOPHOSAURUS SKELETON

Dilophosaurus was a bear-sized, meat-eating dinosaur from Early Jurassic North America. The first skeleton found had semicircular plate-like structures lying near it. Later finds showed that these structures were crests that ran parallel to one another along the length of the skull. However, what no skeleton can ever tell us is what color the crests were in life.

TRIASSIC	EARLY/MID JURASSIC	LATE JURASSIC	EARLY CRETACEOUS	LATE CRETACEOUS
248-206 MYA	206-159 MYA	159-144 MYA	144-97 MYA	97-65 MYA

HEAVY CLAW

Baryonyx was discovered by an amateur fossil collector in southern England in 1983. The skeleton was so complete that it gave us the first clear view of what these animals looked like. *Baryonyx* was an unusual meat-eating dinosaur that had crocodile-like jaws packed with sharp teeth and long forelimbs with hooked claws, which were used to catch fish.

Baryonyx stood 10 feet (3 m) tall, and each of its claws measured nearly 1 foot (35 centimeters) long. We think that it ranged over a large area stretching from England to North Africa.

SPINOSAURUS

MENACING MIMIC

Suchomimus was found in a remote dune-covered area of the Sahara in 1998 by a team from the United States and Niger. A huge predatory dinosaur with a skull like a crocodile's and huge thumb claws, it measured 36 feet (11 m) long and 12 feet (4 m) high at the hip. The thumb claws and powerful forelimbs were used to snare prey, and the thin sail along its back, which reached a height of 2 feet (0.5 m) over the hips, may have been brightly colored for display.

SPINOSAURUS — 50 feet (15 m) long, 24 feet (7 m) high
SUCHOMIMUS — 36 feet (11 m) long, 12 feet (4 m) high
BARYONYX — 32 feet (10 m) long, 10 feet (3 m) high
IRRITATOR — 21 feet (6 m) long, 6 feet (2 m) high

BARYONYX

BIG BITE

Many modern reptiles have features that are similar to those of the spinosaurids. Crocodiles and alligators, for example, have long jaws and many teeth, and they hunt for fish in a similar way. Like the spinosaurids, they were for a long time wrongly suspected of eating their young.

SPINOSAURIDS - THE FISH EATERS

We normally think of fish-eating animals as creatures that live in the water. However, there are many land-living animals that like to eat fish, too. Grizzly bears are often seen beside waterfalls hooking out migrating salmon as they leap to their spawning grounds, and otters live mostly on land but hunt fish. It was the same in the Jurassic Period. One particular family of land-dwelling dinosaurs — the spinosaurids — seems to have been particularly well equipped for fishing. They had long jaws with many small teeth and a big claw on each hand. They lived in Early Cretaceous times, and their remains have been found across the world, from southern England to North Africa and South America.

SUCHOMIMUS

IRRITATOR

SPINY CUSTOMER

Spinosaurus was excavated in Egypt in 1915. Unfortunately, the remains were destroyed when its museum in Germany was bombed in World War II. What we do know about it was that it was as big as *Tyrannosaurus* and had a fin down its back almost 6.5 feet (2 m) tall. The fin was probably used to cool the animal in hot weather. In 1999, a U.S. expedition found its original quarry in Egypt, so there may be hope of finding new specimens.

AN IRRITATING EXAMPLE

Irritator was given its name because of the confusing circumstances in which it was found. The skull — all that we have of the animal — was collected in Brazil sometime in the 1990s and sent to the museum in Stuttgart, Germany. But then the museum staff had a surprise. Whoever dug it up and sold it to the museum had added pieces to it and stuck it together with car body filler to make it look much more spectacular. Now that we have had a good look at it, we can tell that it is a small spinosaurid.

TRIASSIC 248-206 MYA	EARLY/MID JURASSIC 206-159 MYA	LATE JURASSIC 159-144 MYA	EARLY CRETACEOUS 144-97 MYA	LATE CRETACEOUS 97-65 MYA

NQWEBASAURUS

Scientists became very excited in the late 1990s when they found the almost complete skeleton of a 3-foot- (1-m-) long *Nqwebasaurus* embedded in Lower Cretaceous rocks in South Africa. It proved that the family to which most of the small meat-eating dinosaurs belonged (the coelurosaurids) had existed in the southern continents during the Cretaceous period, as well as in North America, Europe, and Asia.

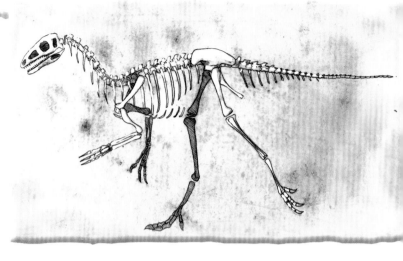

ITALIAN BEAUTY

In the 1990s, this beautifully preserved skeleton of *Scipionyx* was found in Lower Cretaceous rocks in Italy. It was so finely fossilized that even some of the soft anatomy (the lungs and intestines) were preserved. Their existence confirms that this animal, probably along with all other small dinosaurs, was able to breathe efficiently while running. This would have made it an energetic and active hunter. The way the bones were articulated indicates that this specimen of *Scipionyx*, only 10 inches (25 cm) long, was not yet fully grown.

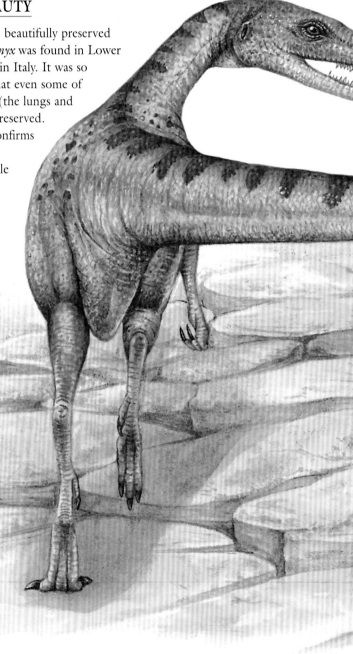

TINIEST FOOTPRINT

In the 1970s, the tiny footprint of a dinosaur that could have been no bigger than a thrush was found in the Upper Triassic rocks of Newfoundland in Canada. The arrangement of the toes is typical of the meat-eating dinosaurs of the Triassic. The print is the only trace we have of the smallest dinosaur ever found. Whether it was a youngster or fully grown, nobody yet knows.

16

THE SMALLEST DINOSAURS

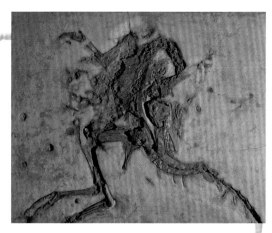

When we think of *dinosaurs* (a name that comes from words meaning "monstrous lizards" or "terrifying lizards"), we usually visualize the huge, fierce animals that have captured our imagination. Some dinosaurs, however, were actually not much bigger than a chicken. Scuttling around among the giants, small dinosaurs were probably more common than big ones. Unfortunately, as their skeletons were so delicate, few have been preserved as fossils. And yet, some good specimens have been found, many preserved in detail.

COMPSOGNATHUS SKELETON

Two *Compsognathus* skeletons have been found: one in France, the other in Germany. The German specimen, which was well preserved in limestone, displays the skeleton and contents of its stomach, showing that its last meal included a small lizard. Some scientists thought *Compsognathus* was the baby of some other dinosaur, but the blobs scattered around the skeleton are probably eggs, proving that this was an adult.

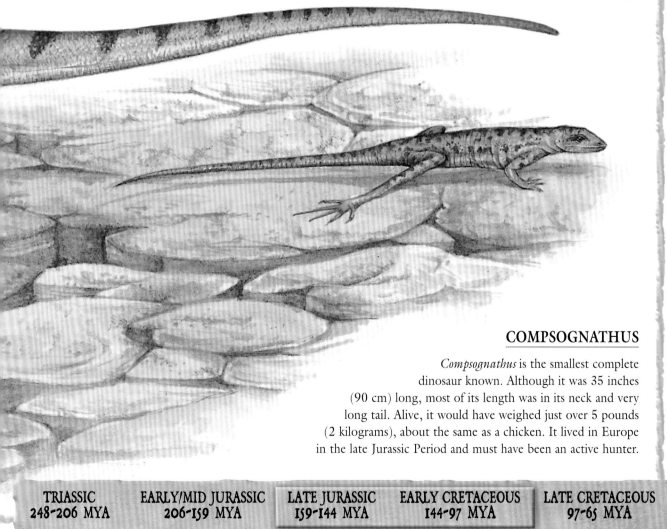

COMPSOGNATHUS

Compsognathus is the smallest complete dinosaur known. Although it was 35 inches (90 cm) long, most of its length was in its neck and very long tail. Alive, it would have weighed just over 5 pounds (2 kilograms), about the same as a chicken. It lived in Europe in the late Jurassic Period and must have been an active hunter.

TRIASSIC 248-206 MYA	EARLY/MID JURASSIC 206-159 MYA	LATE JURASSIC 159-144 MYA	EARLY CRETACEOUS 144-97 MYA	LATE CRETACEOUS 97-65 MYA

JURASSIC GIANT

SKULL

A typical *Allosaurus* skull is about 3.5 feet (1 m) long. The jaws were armed with more than 70 teeth, some measuring 3 inches (8 cm). The teeth were curved, pointed, and serrated, ideal for ripping the flesh of large plant-eating dinosaurs. The joints between the skull bones would have allowed the snout to move up and down to help manipulate food. The lower jaws were hinged so they could expand sideways to allow the animal to gulp down big chunks of meat.

Some dinosaurs really did live up to their reputation of being enormous, fearsome beasts. Probably the most terrifying animal of the Late Jurassic Period was *Allosaurus*. Its remains have been found in the rocks known as the Morrison Formation, which stretches down the western United States from the Canadian border to New Mexico. These deposits yielded the most important dinosaur discoveries made in the second half of the 19th century. Over a hundred different kinds of dinosaur (mostly plant eaters) were found there. The most powerful of the meat eaters found was *Allosaurus*.

MUSCLES

By studying the arrangement of bones in the skeleton and seeing the points of attachment for individual muscles, scientists have figured out what a living *Allosaurus* would have looked like. The leg muscles would have allowed it to move at speeds of up to 18 miles (30 km) per hour — not particularly swift but fast enough to catch the slow-moving herbivores of the time. The neck muscles would have been massive to control the huge head and powerful jaws.

FEET

The feet of *Allosaurus* had three powerful toes, muscular enough to carry the entire weight of the adult, which must have been over a ton. Unlike its fingers, the toes were not equipped with hooked claws but with broad hooves that would have helped bear the great weight. The legs were not particularly long for the size of animal and were evidently not built for speed.

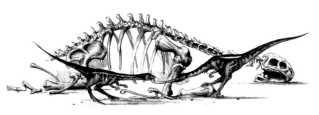

HUNTING

The bones of plant eaters such as *Camarasaurus* are found throughout the Morrison Formation, often mixed up with the broken teeth of meat-eating dinosaurs. Discoveries like these suggest that the big plant eaters — especially sick ones — were often attacked and killed by big meat eaters like *Allosaurus*. Once the killer had eaten its fill, packs of smaller meat eaters (*see pages 10-11*) may have scavenged what was left.

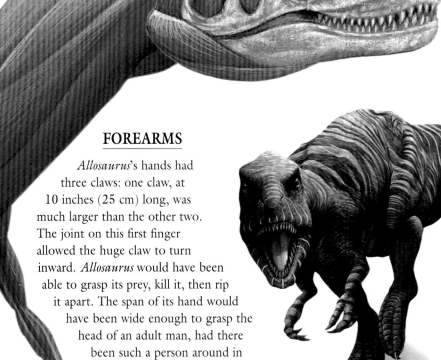

FOREARMS

Allosaurus's hands had three claws: one claw, at 10 inches (25 cm) long, was much larger than the other two. The joint on this first finger allowed the huge claw to turn inward. *Allosaurus* would have been able to grasp its prey, kill it, then rip it apart. The span of its hand would have been wide enough to grasp the head of an adult man, had there been such a person around in Jurassic times!

ALLOSAURUS IN LIFE

We have a fairly good idea what *Allosaurus* looked like from the thousands of bones (some almost complete skeletons) that have been found. These bones belonged to juveniles that measured about 10 feet (3 m) from nose to tail-tip and to adults of about 30 feet (9 m) long. Some of the bones found must have come from 40-foot (12-m) monsters. Mounted casts of *Allosaurus* skeletons can be seen in many museums around the world. The actual bones are too heavy to mount and are usually kept behind the scenes for research.

TRIASSIC 248-206 MYA	EARLY/MID JURASSIC 206-159 MYA	LATE JURASSIC 159-144 MYA	EARLY CRETACEOUS 144-97 MYA	LATE CRETACEOUS 97-65 MYA

FAST HUNTERS

Back in the late 1800s and early 1900s, scientists developed a theory that birds and dinosaurs were related. This theory fell out of favor for a long time but was revived in the 1960s when a group of dinosaurs, extremely birdlike in their build, was discovered. They ranged from the size of a goose to the size of a tiger and had winglike joints in their forearms. They also had strong hind legs with huge, sickle-like killing claws on their feet, showing that they were fast runners and fierce hunters. These dinosaurs are known as the dromaeosaurids (part of a larger group called maniraptorans) and are commonly referred to as "raptors."

BIRD OR DROMAEOSAURID?

Right down to the killing claw on its foot, *Rahonavis*, an Early Cretaceous bird from Madagascar, had the skeleton of a dromaeosaurid. If it had not been for the functional wings, it would have been grouped with the dromaeosaurids.

TERRIBLE CLAWS

The skeleton of a plant-eating *Tenontosaurus*, found in Lower Cretaceous rocks in Montana, was surrounded by the remains of several *Deinonychus*. *Deinonychus* probably hunted in packs, surrounded its prey, and slashed it to death. *Deinonychus* could have stood on one foot and slashed with the other, or it may have hung onto its prey with its clawed hands and slashed away with both hind feet, as cats do.

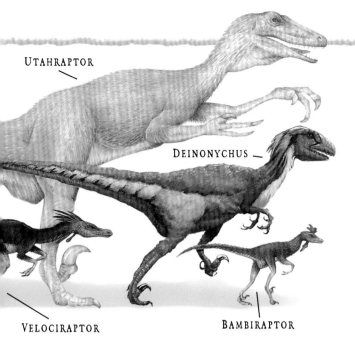

UTAHRAPTOR

DEINONYCHUS —

VELOCIRAPTOR

BAMBIRAPTOR

A RANGE OF DROMAEOSAURIDS

About the size of a goose, *Bambiraptor* is the smallest dromaeosaurid. Turkey-sized *Velociraptor* is probably the best known. Scientists were first alerted to the birdlike nature of these animals in the 1960s, when tiger-sized *Deinonychus* was discovered. Bigger dromaeosaurids are only known from fragments of bone. *Utahraptor* probably weighed more than a ton, while *Megaraptor* (not shown), known only from a 13-inch (34-cm) killing claw, must have approached the size of the big meat eaters, such as *Allosaurus* (*see pages 16–17*). Most of these animals were found in Upper Cretaceous rocks in North America.

EARLY BIRD

This fossil of the first bird *Archaeopteryx*, dating from the Late Jurassic, was found in Germany in 1877. If it had not been for the fossil's feather impressions, the skeleton would have been mistaken for that of a dinosaur because it has a toothed jaw, clawed hands, and a long tail. As well as evolving into modern birds, some of *Archaeopteryx*'s descendants may have lost their powers of flight and developed into meat-eating dromaeosaurids.

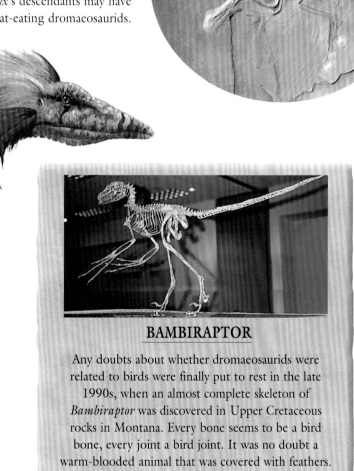

BAMBIRAPTOR

Any doubts about whether dromaeosaurids were related to birds were finally put to rest in the late 1990s, when an almost complete skeleton of *Bambiraptor* was discovered in Upper Cretaceous rocks in Montana. Every bone seems to be a bird bone, every joint a bird joint. It was no doubt a warm-blooded animal that was covered with feathers.

TRIASSIC 248-206 MYA	EARLY/MID JURASSIC 206-159 MYA	LATE JURASSIC 159-144 MYA	EARLY CRETACEOUS 144-97 MYA	LATE CRETACEOUS 97-65 MYA

TROODON

Troodon was one of the maniraptorans, although it was not quite as birdlike as the dromaeosaurids. This small meat eater of the late Cretaceous Period was about 8 feet (2.5 m) long and may well have had feathers.

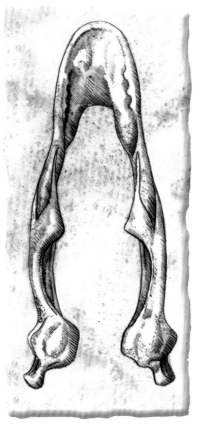

CAENAGNATHUS JAWBONE

Caenagnathus was a dinosaur that probably resembled *Oviraptor* and may have been an egg eater. Certainly, its toothless lower jaw was quite wide in the middle and would have been good for swallowing eggs. As no other remains have been found, *Caenagnathus* remains a bit of a mystery.

OVIRAPTOR HEAD

An *Oviraptor's* head makes it easy to believe it might be an egg eater. Its very short, beaklike mouth and its gullet, situated over the widest part of its jaw, were ideal for swallowing something big and round. As in modern egg-eating snakes, two bones protruding down from its palate were perfectly positioned to tear open an egg on its way down. With its long fingers, which were just right for grasping eggs, *Oviraptor* may have been an egg-eating dinosaur after all. There seems to have been little else for it to eat on the desert plains of Late Cretaceous Mongolia.

EGG THIEF

The jaw of *Caenagnathus* was similar to that of *Chirostenotes*, a turkey-sized dinosaur with very long fingers that would have enabled it to pick up mollusks and insects or raid other dinosaur nests for their eggs. Perhaps there were many different kinds of egg-stealing dinosaurs in Late Cretaceous times.

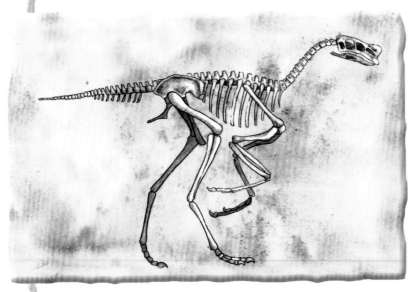

TRIASSIC 248-206 MYA	EARLY/MID JURASSIC 206-159 MYA	LATE JURASSIC 159-144 MYA	EARLY CRETACEOUS 144-97 MYA	LATE CRETACEOUS 97-65 MYA

EGGS & NESTS

Like modern birds, some dinosaurs built nests and laid eggs. The first known dinosaur nests were found by an expedition sent to the Gobi Desert from the American Museum of Natural History in 1923. The nests were among remains of herds of the horned dinosaur *Protoceratops*. Alongside the supposed *Protoceratops* eggs lay the skeleton of a toothless meat eater, *Oviraptor*. This so-called "egg thief" was thought to have been buried in a sandstorm while digging up the eggs. As sometimes happens, however, more evidence caused later paleontologists to re-evaluate this interpretation. In the 1990s, another expedition to the Gobi Desert found the fossil of an *Oviraptor* sitting on a nest, incubating eggs, which meant those first nests must also have been *Oviraptor* nests!

TROODON EGGS

Fossils of *Troodon* nests show they were oval ridges of mud surrounding the eggs, very much like the nests of *Oviraptor*. The eggs were laid in pairs, which suggests that the dinosaur had a pair of oviducts (egg tubes) within its body. A modern bird has only one oviduct. Birds have evolved many such features, which keep down their body weight to make flying easier.

NESTING DINOSAUR

In the 1990s, a fossil of an *Oviraptor* was found sitting on a nest with its arms spread protectively around some eggs, evidently keeping them warm with its body heat. Modern birds do this, since their feathers provide insulation. This is one piece of evidence suggesting that *Oviraptor*, and many other birdlike dinosaurs, had feathers.

BIRD OR DINOSAUR?

As well as finding the first dinosaur nests, the U.S. expeditions to the Gobi Desert in the 1920s uncovered many other dinosaur remains. One of these that we now call *Mononykus* was a total puzzle. Was it a bird or was it a dinosaur? If it was a bird, its arms were too short for it to fly. If it was a dinosaur, what good were hands reduced to a single finger with a big claw? In the 1980s, when new specimens were discovered, *Mononykus* was found to have belonged to a group of related animals, the alvarezsaurids — a distinct group within the maniraptorans — that ranged from South America to Central Asia. Today, we still do not know whether they were birds or dinosaurs.

MONONYKUS

The best known and most complete of the alvarezsaurids was *Mononykus*. It looked like a very lightly built, meat-eating dinosaur with spindly legs and a long tail. The two forelimbs are remarkable. They are short and have a shelf of bone, which in modern birds would support wing feathers, and each bears a single stout, stubby claw. These forelimbs probably evolved from the functional wings of a flying ancestor, such as the Late Jurassic *Archaeopteryx*.

OSTRICH

One function of non-flying wings in modern running birds is for display. The ostrich makes a big show of its wing feathers when it is courting a mate or threatening an enemy. It is quite possible that the part-bird/part-dinosaur animals of the Cretaceous Period also had flamboyant feathers on their flightless wings and used them for display. Unfortunately, such behavior cannot be proven by fossil evidence.

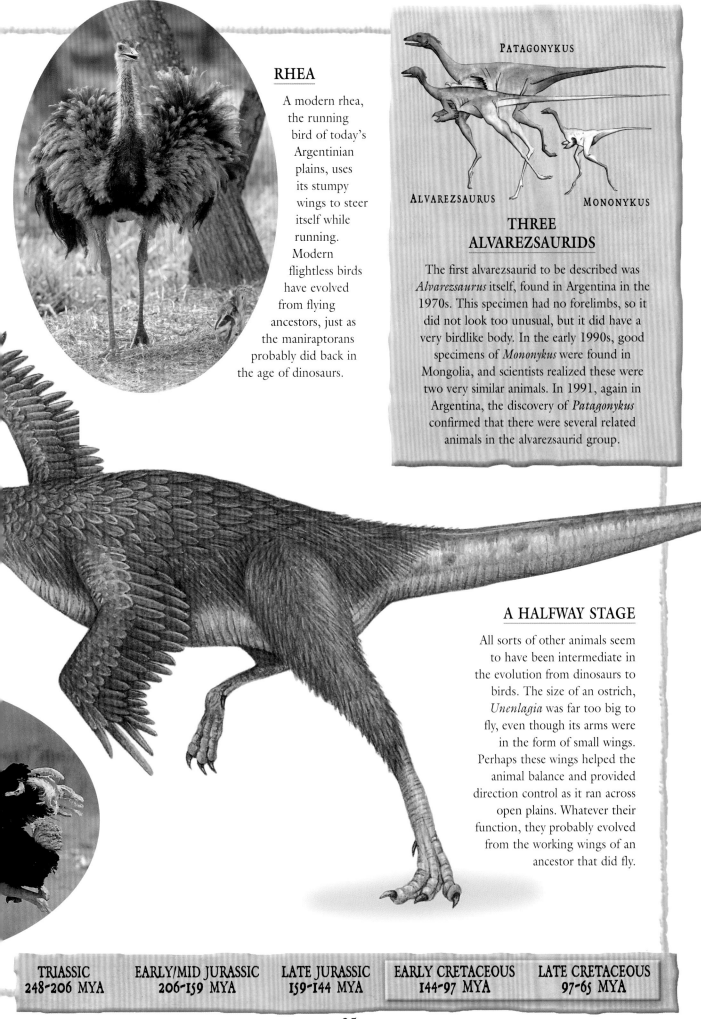

RHEA

A modern rhea, the running bird of today's Argentinian plains, uses its stumpy wings to steer itself while running. Modern flightless birds have evolved from flying ancestors, just as the maniraptorans probably did back in the age of dinosaurs.

THREE ALVAREZSAURIDS

PATAGONYKUS

ALVAREZSAURUS

MONONYKUS

The first alvarezsaurid to be described was *Alvarezsaurus* itself, found in Argentina in the 1970s. This specimen had no forelimbs, so it did not look too unusual, but it did have a very birdlike body. In the early 1990s, good specimens of *Mononykus* were found in Mongolia, and scientists realized these were two very similar animals. In 1991, again in Argentina, the discovery of *Patagonykus* confirmed that there were several related animals in the alvarezsaurid group.

A HALFWAY STAGE

All sorts of other animals seem to have been intermediate in the evolution from dinosaurs to birds. The size of an ostrich, *Unenlagia* was far too big to fly, even though its arms were in the form of small wings. Perhaps these wings helped the animal balance and provided direction control as it ran across open plains. Whatever their function, they probably evolved from the working wings of an ancestor that did fly.

TRIASSIC 248-206 MYA	EARLY/MID JURASSIC 206-159 MYA	LATE JURASSIC 159-144 MYA	EARLY CRETACEOUS 144-97 MYA	LATE CRETACEOUS 97-65 MYA

TERRIBLE HAND

An intriguing fossil from Late Cretaceous rocks in Mongolia shows a pair of arms, 8 feet (2.5 m) long, with three-clawed hands. The animal has been given the name *Deinocheirus,* but we know nothing else about it. The bones look as if they are from an ornithomimid, but they are far bigger than those of any known member of this group. For now, the owner of these extraordinary bones remains a mystery.

GALLIMIMUS SKELETON

Gallimimus, probably the best known of the ornithomimids, had a small, toothless beak. This dinosaur was built for speed and could run at up to 50 miles (80 km) per hour, as fast as a race horse. It usually paced around slowly, stalking small mammals or snapping up seeds and insects, but its speed meant that it could escape from most predators. Its long tail acted as a counterbalance to the front of the body, propelling it forward while it sprinted. Its hipbone also pointed forward. This skeleton is on display at the Natural History Museum in London.

Struthiomimus

ORNITHOMIMIDS

All ornithomimids looked similar but varied somewhat in size. *Struthiomimus* was about the size of an ostrich. *Pelecanimimus* was one of the earliest. It had a pouch of skin beneath its long jaws, which had hundreds of tiny teeth. This suggests that the teeth of the group became smaller and smaller before disappearing altogether in the later ornithomimids. *Garidumimus,* named after a mythical Hindu bird, had a small crest on its head. The biggest known was *Gallimimus,* the "chicken mimic" at 13–16 feet (4–5 m) long. Some chicken!

TRIASSIC 248-206 MYA	EARLY/MID JURASSIC 206-159 MYA	LATE JURASSIC 159-144 MYA	EARLY CRETACEOUS 144-97 MYA	LATE CRETACEOUS 97-65 MYA

BIRD MIMICS

One group of dinosaurs has always been thought to look very much like birds. Ornithomimids ("bird mimics") had plump, compact bodies; big eyes; toothless beaks on small heads that were supported on long, slender necks; and long legs with thick muscles close to the hip. Typical of the group was *Struthiomimus* ("ostrich mimic") from the Late Cretaceous. Although they fall into the category of meat-eating dinosaurs and would have descended from purely carnivorous ancestors, these dinosaurs were probably omnivorous, eating fruit and leaves as well as insects and small vertebrates, such as lizards. Ostriches and other ground birds of today are also omnivores.

BUILT FOR SPEED

As with most meat-eating dinosaurs, the skeleton of an ornithomimid, such as this *Ornithomimus*, is very birdlike. Balanced by its long tail, its head would have been held farther forward than that of an ostrich. However, it had very similar legs, with a very short femur (thighbone) that would have held all the muscles so the lower leg and the toes were worked only by tendons. This gives a very lightweight leg that could move quickly — a good running leg.

GALLIMIMUS

GARIDUMIMUS

PELECANIMIMUS

EMU

A modern emu is a plains-living animal. The keen eyes in the head, held high on top of a long neck, can spot danger from far across open spaces. Its strong running legs can take it out of danger at great speed. Because of the physical similarity, we think the Late Cretaceous ornithomimids had a similar life on the plains of North America and central Asia.

ERLIKOSAURUS SKULL

The only known segnosaurid skull is that of *Erlikosaurus*. It looks very much like the skulls of some of the big plant-eating dinosaurs. Behind its toothless beak, the teeth are small and leaf shaped. Some scientists have suggested that this might be the skull of a fish-eating dinosaur and that the foot bones (which are also unusual) could have been webbed for swimming. However, the rest of the skeleton suggests that it could not have been a swimming animal.

SEGNOSAURUS HIPBONE

The hipbones of meat-eating dinosaurs are usually distinctive. The pubis bone at the front points forward. In the segnosaurids, however, this bone sweeps backward. This is usually only seen in plant-eating dinosaurs, as it gives more space for the big plant-eating intestines that such animals need. Such a pubis bone would have given a segnosaurid's body a very dumpy appearance. This is part of what makes the whole group a puzzle.

SEGNOSAURIDS

Sometimes, part of a skeleton is so unlike any known dinosaur that nobody knows what kind it is. Such is the case with segnosaurids. In the 1920s, the first bones, found in Upper Cretaceous rocks in Mongolia, were thought to be from a giant turtle, but they were reclassified as dinosaur remains in the 1970s. The various bits of bone were so unalike that they seemed to be from different families of dinosaur. Even now, the name therizinosaurid is sometimes used for the group. This name was first used as the original classification of the forelimb, as opposed to segnosaurid, the name chosen when the skull and backbone were studied. These dinosaurs were classified as meat eaters, then as prosauropods, one of the long-necked plant eaters. For the time being, at least, they are back with the meat eaters.

A MODERN PARALLEL

The anteater is a modern animal with claws that seem too big for its body. It uses them to rip through the tough walls of anthills to get at the ant colony. Some scientists have suggested that this is how segnosaurids lived.

TRIASSIC 248-206 MYA	EARLY/MID JURASSIC 206-159 MYA	LATE JURASSIC 159-144 MYA	EARLY CRETACEOUS 144-97 MYA	LATE CRETACEOUS 97-65 MYA

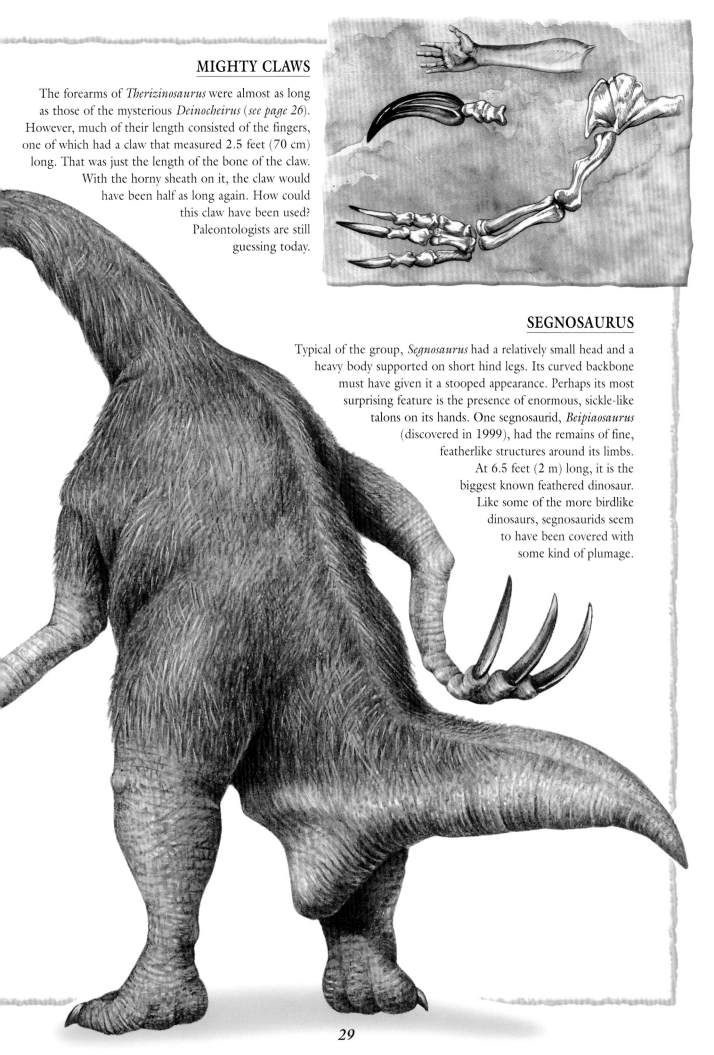

MIGHTY CLAWS

The forearms of *Therizinosaurus* were almost as long as those of the mysterious *Deinocheirus* (*see page 26*). However, much of their length consisted of the fingers, one of which had a claw that measured 2.5 feet (70 cm) long. That was just the length of the bone of the claw. With the horny sheath on it, the claw would have been half as long again. How could this claw have been used? Paleontologists are still guessing today.

SEGNOSAURUS

Typical of the group, *Segnosaurus* had a relatively small head and a heavy body supported on short hind legs. Its curved backbone must have given it a stooped appearance. Perhaps its most surprising feature is the presence of enormous, sickle-like talons on its hands. One segnosaurid, *Beipiaosaurus* (discovered in 1999), had the remains of fine, featherlike structures around its limbs. At 6.5 feet (2 m) long, it is the biggest known feathered dinosaur. Like some of the more birdlike dinosaurs, segnosaurids seem to have been covered with some kind of plumage.

FOOTPRINT

In the late 1980s, a dinosaur footprint almost 3 feet (1 m) long was discovered on a slab of Upper Cretaceous rock in New Mexico. Whatever beast made the print had the claws of a meat eater. There was only one print, so the stride of the animal must have been greater than the almost 10-foot- (3-m-) long slab of rock. Scientists say the animal was moving at 5–6 miles (8–10 km) per hour. We cannot be sure this footprint was made by *Tyrannosaurus*, but we know of no bigger meat-eating dinosaurs in Cretaceous America.

TYRANNOSAURIDS

At 39 feet (12 m) long and 20 feet (6 m) tall, *Tyrannosaurus* must have been the scourge of the North American continent at the end of the dinosaur age. So far, about 15 specimens of *Tyrannosaurus* have been discovered in various states of completeness. From these we have a picture of what the mighty beasts looked like. However, there is still much debate about how they lived. Some scientists think they actively hunted, perhaps waiting in ambush for duckbills, the big plant eaters of the time, then charging out at them from the cover of the forest. Others insist they were too big for such activity but would have scavenged carrion, the meat of already-dead animals. Maybe they did both.

A RANGE OF TYRANNOSAURIDS

Daspletosaurus from North America was similar to *Tyrannosaurus* but was a little smaller and had a heavy head with fewer but larger teeth. At about 20 feet (6 m) long, *Alioramus* was a medium-sized tyrannosaurid from Asia. It had a long skull with knobbles and spikes along the top. The smallest was *Nanotyrannus*, from Montana, at 13 feet (4 m) long. Experts are undecided about this last one. Some think it may have been a small *Albertosaurus*.

NANOTYRANNUS

FRIGHTFUL BITE

Tyrannosaurus had incredibly powerful jaws and teeth used to rip flesh from its prey. Gouges in the pelvic bone of a Late Cretaceous specimen of the three-horned dinosaur *Triceratops* exactly match the size and spacing of the teeth of *Tyrannosaurus*. From these marks, scientists could tell that a *Tyrannosaurus* bit down into the meat of the hind leg and tore it away from the bone when the *Triceratops* was already dead. But whether it was the *Tyrannosaurus* that killed it, nobody can tell.

TYRANT LIZARD KING

Tyrannosaurus, the biggest of the tyrannosaurids, is often known by its full species name *Tyrannosaurus rex* or simply *T. rex*. Other dinosaurs also have full species names, such as *Allosaurus atrox*, *Velociraptor mongoliensis*, and so on, but these are usually only used by scientists.

DASPLETOSAURUS

ALIORAMUS

COPROLITE

Fossilized animal droppings are known to geologists as coprolites, and they give useful clues to an extinct animal's diet. As with footprints, however, it is often impossible to tell what animal made which coprolite. Big coprolites, more than 8 inches (20 cm) long, that may have come from *Tyrannosaurus*, have been found to contain smashed, undigested bone fragments.

TRIASSIC 248-206 MYA	EARLY/MID JURASSIC 206-159 MYA	LATE JURASSIC 159-144 MYA	EARLY CRETACEOUS 144-97 MYA	LATE CRETACEOUS 97-65 MYA

MONSTROUS SKULL

The skull of *Carcharodontosaurus* is almost completely known. When putting the skull bones together, the scientists only had to recreate the missing front of the snout and the bones at the very rear. This they could do by drawing on their knowledge of other skulls. The final skull is 5 feet (1.5 m) long and has strong, curved, shark-like teeth. We know far less about the skull of *Giganotosaurus*. What we can be sure of is that the jaws were not as powerful as those of *Tyrannosaurus*, the teeth were not as strong, and it had an even smaller brain than the Tyrant Lizard King.

CARCHARODONTOSAURUS

Related to the Jurassic *Allosaurus* (*see pages 18-19*), *Carcharodontosaurus* came from Morocco, in North Africa. Some fossils of this creature were discovered by a German expedition in 1925, but they were destroyed when their museum was bombed during World War II, along with the original remains of *Spinosaurus* found on the same expedition. Only when more fossils were discovered in the mid-1990s did paleontologists realize that *Carcharodontosaurus* was a 50-foot-(15-m-) long giant.

TRIASSIC 248-206 MYA	EARLY/MID JURASSIC 206-159 MYA	LATE JURASSIC 159-144 MYA	EARLY CRETACEOUS 144-97 MYA	LATE CRETACEOUS 97-65 MYA

THE NEW KINGS

What was the biggest, strongest, and fiercest meat-eating dinosaur that ever lived? *Tyrannosaurus*? Not any more! For the past hundred years we have said that *Tyrannosaurus* was the most powerful of the meat-eating dinosaurs. Generations of scientists have believed this to be so and have even stated that it would be mechanically impossible for bigger meat-eating animals to have existed. But now, the remains of even bigger meat eaters are being found. In the 1990s, the skeletons of two carnivorous dinosaurs were found within a year of one another: one in South America, the other in Africa. Although neither skeleton was complete, they appear to have belonged to a group of dinosaurs that were even longer than *Tyrannosaurus*.

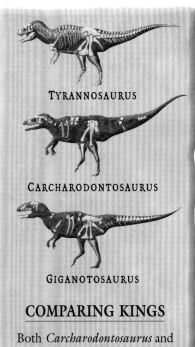

TYRANNOSAURUS

CARCHARODONTOSAURUS

GIGANOTOSAURUS

COMPARING KINGS

Both *Carcharodontosaurus* and *Giganotosaurus* were longer than the previous record-holder, *Tyrannosaurus*. As shown above, however, only *Tyrannosaurus* is known from complete skeletons, and there is still a lot we don't know about the other two. Even so, *Tyrannosaurus* seems to have been a much heavier animal and was higher at the hip, so we could still say that the biggest meat-eating dinosaur that is completely known is *Tyrannosaurus*. Still the king!

GIGANOTOSAURUS

The great meat-eating dinosaur *Giganotosaurus* seems to have been closely related to *Carcharodontosaurus,* even though it lived in isolated South America in the Late Cretaceous Period, while the other lived in Africa. It is likely that in the early part of the Cretaceous Period, before the continents were separated by oceans, the ancestors of these animals spread across the whole world. After the continents split apart, *Giganotosaurus* began to evolve separately.

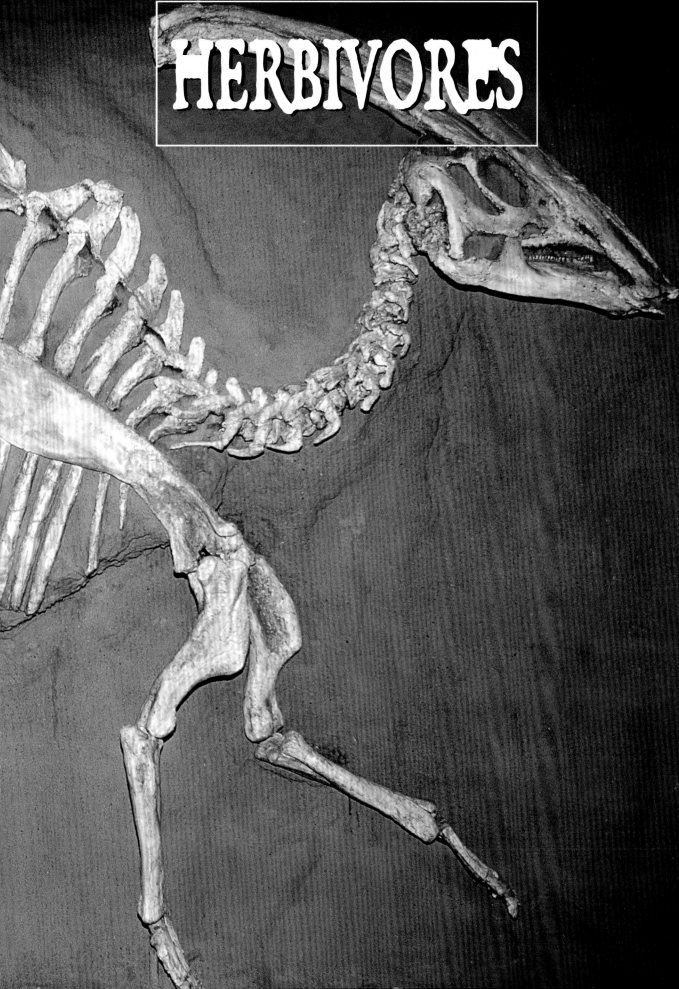

HERBIVORES

MUSSAURUS

The smallest dinosaur skeleton known belongs to a prosauropod. This *Mussaurus* is small enough to be held in the the palm of a human hand. We know it is the skeleton of a baby or an embryo, however, because the eyes and feet are bigger in relation to its body size than they would be in an adult, and its bones are not totally fused together. An adult *Mussaurus* would have been about 10 feet (3 meters) long.

SKULL COMPARISON BETWEEN A HERBIVORE AND CARNIVORE

PLATEOSAURUS

- *Jaw articulates below level of teeth.*
- *Leaf-shaped teeth with continuous cutting edge.*
- *Coarsely serrated teeth for shredding leaves and shoots.*
- *Teeth more or less the same size.*
- *No gaps between teeth.*

TYRANNOSAURUS

- *Jaw articulates at point level with teeth.*
- *Strong, spike-shaped, piercing teeth used for gripping and killing.*
- *Finely serrated saw-edged teeth like a steak knife.*
- *Teeth often break off and new ones grow in their place, creating a snaggle-toothed appearance.*
- *Teeth have gaps between them.*

DINOSAURS

RHYNCHOSAURS

MAMMAL-LIKE REPTILES

DEVELOPING VEGETATION

In the early part of the age of reptiles, the most prolific plant, a fern with seeds, was the primary food source of the main plant-eating animals, the mammal-like reptiles. The seed ferns died away during the Triassic Period, and ferns more like our modern species became common. Another group, the rhynchosaurs, evolved to eat them. At the end of the Triassic, conifer trees spread everywhere, and prosauropod dinosaurs evolved to eat them.

THE FIRST PLANT-EATING DINOSAURS

Plant-eating dinosaurs (herbivores) were the real giants of the Mesozoic Era. Among their ranks were the mighty *Diplodocus* and *Seisomosaurus*, the largest animals ever to walk our planet. Herbivorous reptiles are known from the early part of the Carboniferous Period, 350 million years ago. The first herbivorous dinosaurs evolved in the Late Triassic Period, appearing about the same time as carnivores. Because both groups of dinosaurs have similarly formed hipbones, we know that the plant eaters are closely related to meat-eating dinosaurs.

PANGAEA

The world was very different in Late Triassic/Early Jurassic times. All the continental landmasses were together in one area, called Pangaea. This meant that animals of the same kind could migrate everywhere and is why we find the remains of almost identical animals all over the world, from Australia to North America.

PLATEOSAURUS

The first plant-eating dinosaurs belonged to the prosauropod group. *Plateosaurus* was a typical prosauropod. It had a long neck and small head, but perhaps its most important feature was its big body. To process plant matter, a herbivore needs a far greater digestive system than a carnivore. The prosauropod's heavy mass of intestines, carried well forward of the hips, would have made the animal too unbalanced to spend much time on its hind legs, so prosauropods became four-footers early in their history.

TRIASSIC 248-206 MYA	EARLY/MID JURASSIC 206-159 MYA	LATE JURASSIC 159-144 MYA	EARLY CRETACEOUS 144-99 MYA	LATE CRETACEOUS 99-65 MYA

HELPLESS PREY

Paleontologists have found the remains of a prosauropod *Euskelosaurus* in Upper Triassic rocks in South Africa and Switzerland. The bones of its feet and legs are preserved, but the rest of the skeleton is broken up and scattered. Teeth of crocodile-like reptiles and carnivorous dinosaurs are among them. From this we suppose that *Euskelosaurus* became stuck in mud and, while struggling helplessly, was attacked by meat eaters.

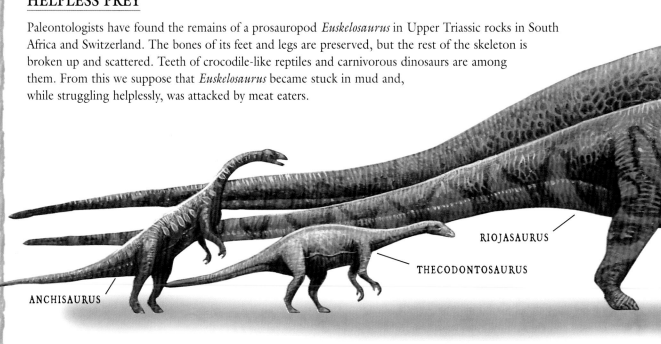

ANCHISAURUS

THECODONTOSAURUS

RIOJASAURUS

LIFE OF THE PROSAUROPODS

Ever since plants have existed, plant-eating animals have fed on them, and ever since plant-eating animals have existed, meat eaters have, in turn, fed on them. This type of food chain can still be seen on the grasslands of Africa, where herds of herbivorous wildebeest and zebra graze on low vegetation and are preyed on by prowling carnivores such as lions and cheetahs. It was no different with dinosaurs. Prosauropods fed on the trees and were themselves stalked by meat eaters.

TRACKWAYS

The footprints called *Navajopus* from Lower Jurassic rocks of Arizona perfectly match the foot bones of a typical prosauropod, with big hind feet and smaller front feet, each with four toes and inwardly curved claws. They are likely to have been made by a small *Thecodontosaurus*-sized prosauropod called *Ammosaurus*.

MELANOROSAURUS

RANGE OF PROSAUROPODS

During the Triassic Period, sauropods ranged all over Pangaea, the world's landmass. *Melanorosaurus* lived in South Africa, *Thecodontosaurus* in western Europe, *Anchisaurus* in western North America, and *Riojasaurus* in South America. Other prosauropods, such as *Plateosaurus* and the *Plateosaurus*-like *Lufengosaurus*, lived in what is now China. They were all extinct by Middle Jurassic times.

TRIASSIC 248-206 MYA	EARLY/MID JURASSIC 206-159 MYA	LATE JURASSIC 159-144 MYA	EARLY CRETACEOUS 144-99 MYA	LATE CRETACEOUS 99-65 MYA

SAUROPODS

STOMACH STONES

The small head and mouth of sauropods were not designed for chewing. To help break down food, they swallowed stones, which ground up plant material. We know this because gastroliths (stomach stones) have been found among their bones. Today, many plant-eating birds do the same.

The biggest dinosaurs were long-necked plant eaters known as sauropods ("lizard feet"). They had elephantine bodies, legs like tree trunks, small heads on top of long necks, and long, whiplike tails. They were related to the meat-eating dinosaurs and to the prosauropods, evolving in the Early Jurassic and dying off in Cretaceous times.

DIPLODOCUS

Perhaps the best known of the long sauropods is *Diplodocus*. At 88 feet (27 m) long, it was one of several sauropods that roamed North America in Late Jurassic times. The way the neck bones were articulated tells us they browsed on low ferny vegetation, probably sweeping out great arcs with their long necks.

SAUROPOD FRAME

Remains of sauropod skeletons consist of massive pieces of fossilized bone, so big there is nothing alive today that compares with them. In one of the latest techniques, very basic bone shapes are programmed into a computer and manipulated to let us see how the various pieces moved against one another.

TRACES OF LIFESTYLE

We used to think sauropods were too heavy to spend much time on land and must have supported their vast bulk by wading in deep water. However, we now know (mostly from fossilized footprints) that sauropods moved about in herds on dry land. Large and small footprints found together show that different sauropods lived in groups. Because there is no sign of tail marks in the tracks, they must have kept their tails raised.

SHUNOSAURUS

DIPLODOCUS

IN DEFENSE

Sauropods would have been prey to the big carnivorous dinosaurs. Just as today tigers do not attack fully grown elephants, in Jurassic times the biggest of the sauropods would have been safe from the meat eaters, but the young and the sick would have been under constant threat. *Diplodocus* probably protected itself and its herd by using its long tapering tail as a whip. *Shunosaurus*, which lived in China during the Middle Jurassic, probably used the small club on the end of its tail to defend itself.

TRIASSIC	EARLY/MID JURASSIC	LATE JURASSIC	EARLY CRETACEOUS	LATE CRETACEOUS
248-206 MYA	206-159 MYA	159-144 MYA	144-99 MYA	99-65 MYA

APATOSAURUS GROWTH RATE

It is difficult to tell how long a dinosaur lived. Sometimes, growth lines in the bones (like the rings of trees) suggest the animal grew more quickly at some time each year. Its age can be assessed by counting the lines. Studies of the bones of *Apatosaurus* (previously known as *Brontosaurus*), a relative of *Diplodocus*, suggest these sauropods grew quickly, without growth rings, for about 10 years. By then, they had reached 90 percent of their adult size.

10 YEARS

BRACHIOSAURUS

Although many remains have been found in the Morrison Formation, the best skeleton of *Brachiosaurus* was found halfway across the globe in Tanzania. This shows that in Late Jurassic times, Pangaea (*see pages 36-37*) had not yet split completely and the same types of dinosaur lived all over the world. A German expedition unearthed this skeleton in 1909, when Tanzania was known as German East Africa. The complete skeleton, the biggest mounted anywhere, is in the Humboldt Museum in Berlin.

TRIASSIC 248-206 MYA	EARLY/MID JURASSIC 206-159 MYA	LATE JURASSIC 159-144 MYA	EARLY CRETACEOUS 144-99 MYA	LATE CRETACEOUS 99-65 MYA

THE HEYDAY OF THE SAUROPODS

During the Late Jurassic, sauropods were at their most widespread. Some were long and low and browsed low vegetation. Others were tall and browsed lower branches of trees. There were two main types, as distinguished by the shape of their teeth. *Diplodocus* and the other long, low sauropods had peglike teeth, while the taller, stouter sauropods, such as *Brachiosaurus*, had thick, spoon-shaped teeth that indicate a different type of feeding arrangement. However, nobody is sure what it was.

DINOSAUR DETECTIVES

Often, when the remains of a very big animal are discovered, there are tantalizingly few bones found. Comparing them directly to a more complete skeleton can give us some idea of the kind of animal they came from. In 1999, four neck vertebrae of a gigantic sauropod were found. The *Sauroposeidon* bones turned out to be very similar to the neck bones of *Brachiosaurus*. So we are fairly sure *Sauroposeidon* was an animal very much like *Brachiosaurus* — but bigger!

SEISMOSAURUS

The longest dinosaur known is *Seismosaurus*. Imagine *Diplodocus*, then double its length. Make this length by stretching the neck and the tail in proportion to the body, and this is what *Seismosaurus* looked like. So far, only one *Seismosaurus* skeleton has been found, and that was in the Morrison Formation rocks in New Mexico. The skeleton is of an animal that may have been about 164 feet (50 m) long.

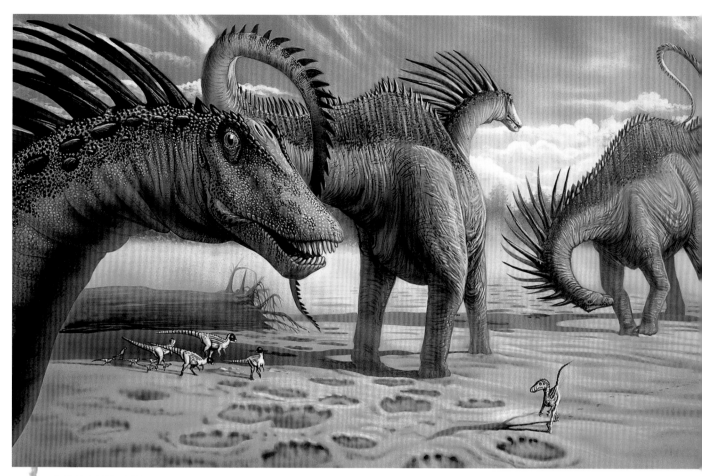

DRESSED TO IMPRESS

Not only did late sauropods have armor, but some had spines and frills as well. *Amargasaurus* from Early Cretaceous Argentina had a double row of spines down its neck and a tall fin down its back. Unusual sauropods evolved in Cretaceous South America because it was an island continent, and evolution took an independent direction.

ARGENTINOSAURUS

So far, the heaviest dinosaur ever found is *Argentinosaurus*. We have only six vertebrae, a part of its hips, a bit of rib, and a leg bone. The leg bone is as tall as a man. From this we believe the animal was about 88 feet (27 m) long and weighed about 55 tons. Like some earlier Morrison Formation sauropods, *Argentinosaurus* had vertebrae made of thin struts and sheets of bone with great hollows between them — a strong but light construction vital for a huge animal.

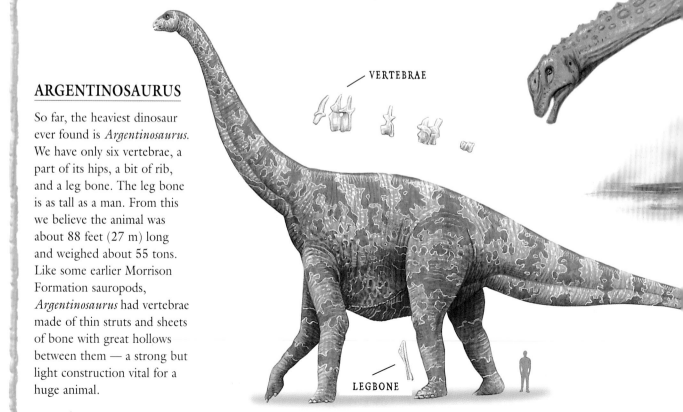

VERTEBRAE

LEGBONE

THE LAST OF THE SAUROPODS

As the world passed from the Jurassic into the Cretaceous Period, vegetation began to change and the continents moved apart. Different dinosaurs were becoming prominent. The sauropods began to die away as a completely different group of plant-eating dinosaurs evolved. In some places, the sauropods still thrived, either because the old style vegetation still flourished in some environments or because they lived on isolated continents where the new dinosaurs did not reach. Despite the spread of the new dinosaur types, there were sauropods existing to the very end of the Mesozoic Era.

TOUGH GUY

The bony armor pieces from the back of a titanosaurid were found as long ago as 1890 in Madagascar. The paleontologist who first identified them was not believed, because no other sauropod was known to be covered with armor. Only with the discovery of armored titanosaurids in Argentina in the 1970s and a more complete armored titanosaurid in Madagascar in the 1990s was this scientist's theory proven correct.

SALTASAURUS

Of the sauropods that survived into the Cretaceous Period, the titanosaurids (such as *Saltasaurus* in Argentina or *Ampelosaurus* in France) were perhaps the most successful. Despite their name, at about 39 feet (12 m) long, they were not particularly big for sauropods. In recent years, it has been found that at least some titanosaurids had a back covered with armor. This may not have been for defense; like the shell on the back of a crab, it might have been for stiffening the backbone to help the animal carry its weight.

TRIASSIC 248-206 MYA	EARLY/MID JURASSIC 206-159 MYA	LATE JURASSIC 159-144 MYA	EARLY CRETACEOUS 144-99 MYA	LATE CRETACEOUS 99-65 MYA

ORNITHOPODS - THE BIRD FEET

HYPSILOPHODON SKULL

The skull of an ornithopod was different from that of a sauropod. There was always a beak at the front for cropping food. The teeth were not merely for raking in leaves but were designed for chewing them, either by chopping or grinding. Depressions at each side of the skull show where there were probably cheek pouches used to hold the food while it was being processed. This is a far more complicated arrangement than that of the prosauropods and sauropods.

During the Triassic, at about the same time as meat eaters and prosauropods appeared, another group of plant eaters appeared. What made them different was their hipbones, which gave more space to the big intestines plant eaters needed yet enabled them to balance on their hind legs. Scientists in the 1800s called these plant eaters sauropods ("lizard feet") because they had a lizard-like arrangement of bones in their feet; the two-footed, bird-hipped dinosaurs they called ornithopods ("bird feet").

ADVANCED JAWS

Later, more advanced ornithopods had complex chewing mechanisms. An animal like *Iguanodon* (*see page 49*) or a hadrosaur (*see pages 50-51*) had its upper teeth mounted on articulated plates at each side of the skull. As the lower jaw rose, these plates moved outward to allow the sloping chewing surfaces of both sets of teeth to grind past one another. This constant milling action wore away the teeth, and new ones grew to replace them.

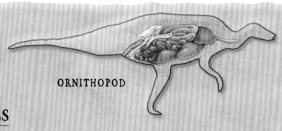

SAUROPOD   ORNITHOPOD

HIPBONES

As with the prosauropods (*see pages 38–39*), the hipbones of the sauropods incorporated a pubic bone that pointed down and forward. This meant the big plant-digesting intestines had to be carried forward of the hips. In ornithopods, this pubic bone is swept back, except for a pair of forward extensions that splayed out to the side. The big plant-digesting intestines could be carried beneath the animal's hipbone, closer to its center of gravity. This enabled the ornithopod to walk on its hind legs, balanced by its tail — just like a meat-eating dinosaur.

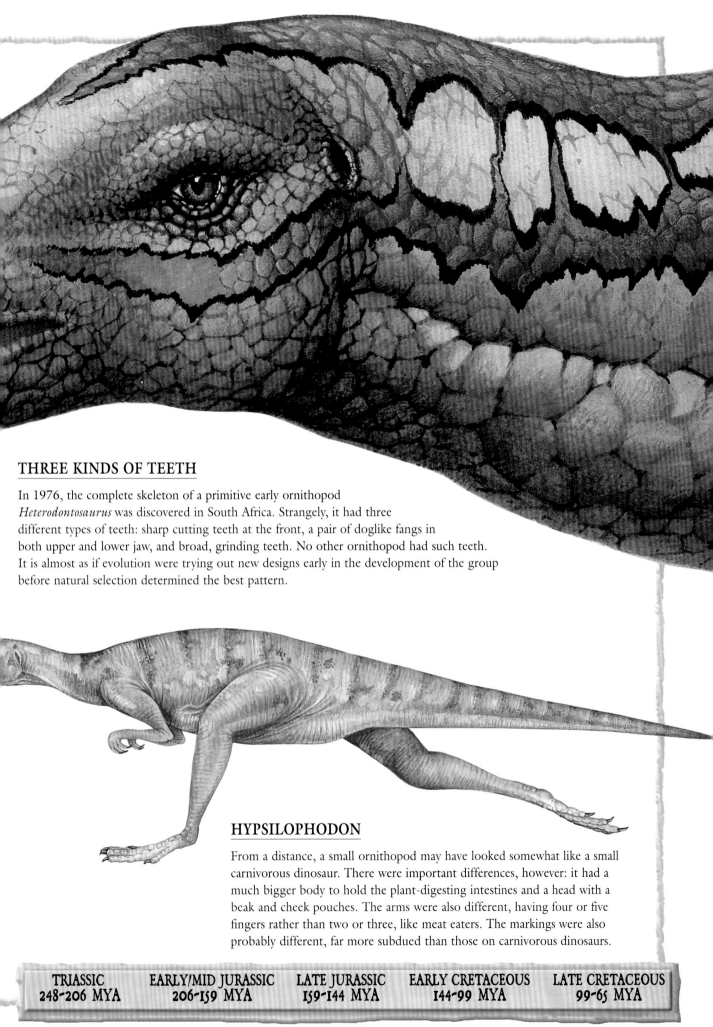

THREE KINDS OF TEETH

In 1976, the complete skeleton of a primitive early ornithopod
Heterodontosaurus was discovered in South Africa. Strangely, it had three
different types of teeth: sharp cutting teeth at the front, a pair of doglike fangs in
both upper and lower jaw, and broad, grinding teeth. No other ornithopod had such teeth.
It is almost as if evolution were trying out new designs early in the development of the group
before natural selection determined the best pattern.

HYPSILOPHODON

From a distance, a small ornithopod may have looked somewhat like a small
carnivorous dinosaur. There were important differences, however: it had a
much bigger body to hold the plant-digesting intestines and a head with a
beak and cheek pouches. The arms were also different, having four or five
fingers rather than two or three, like meat eaters. The markings were also
probably different, far more subdued than those on carnivorous dinosaurs.

TRIASSIC 248-206 MYA	EARLY/MID JURASSIC 206-159 MYA	LATE JURASSIC 159-144 MYA	EARLY CRETACEOUS 144-99 MYA	LATE CRETACEOUS 99-65 MYA

CHANGING FACE

Over the years, as more specimens were found, *Iguanodon*'s appearance changed. In the 1850s, it was constructed in the Crystal Palace gardens in London, along the lines of Mantell's big lizard. Then, in 1878, a whole herd of *Iguanodon* skeletons, mostly complete, were found in a coal mine in Bernissart, Belgium. These animals were up to 33 feet (10 m) long and had hind legs that were much longer than their forelimbs. This evidence led to reconstructions of *Iguanodon* sitting on its hind legs, resting on its tail like a kangaroo — an image that was accepted for the next century.

IGUANA TOOTH

The first remains of *Iguanodon* — teeth and parts of bones — were discovered in Kent in about 1822 by English country doctor Gideon Mantell and his wife, Mary. Other scientists of the day thought they were the teeth of fish, or of a hippopotamus. But Mantell realized the teeth were from a plant-eating reptile like a modern iguana lizard. His first reconstructions showed a kind of a dragon-sized, iguana-like reptile, similar to the first reconstructions of the meat-eating *Megalosaurus*, also recently discovered.

MUTTABURRASAURUS

TENONTOSAURUS

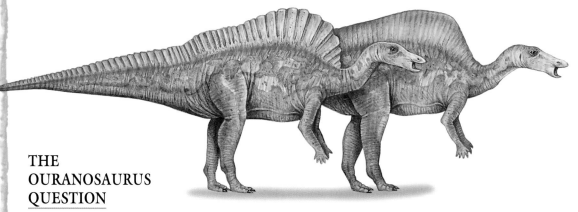

THE OURANOSAURUS QUESTION

One iguanodontid, *Ouranosaurus*, had an arrangement of tall spines forming a kind of picket fence along its backbone, probably to support some sort of fin or sail. Since *Ouranosaurus* lived in North Africa, which was hot and arid during Cretaceous times, such a sail could have regulated its body temperature by exposing blood vessels to the warming sun and cooling wind. A meat eater, *Spinosaurus,* lived in the same time and place and also had a sail. Another theory is that the spines supported a fatty hump, such as camels have today.

THE IGUANODON DYNASTY

Iguanodon was among the first dinosaurs to be discovered. The teeth and a few scraps of bone were found first and were obviously from a large plant-eating reptile. At the time, few people were familiar with modern plant-eating reptiles, so the animal was particularly unusual. Some scientific work was being done on the modern South American plant-eating lizard, the iguana, which had teeth somewhat like those of this new fossil. Hence, it was given the name *Iguanodon*.

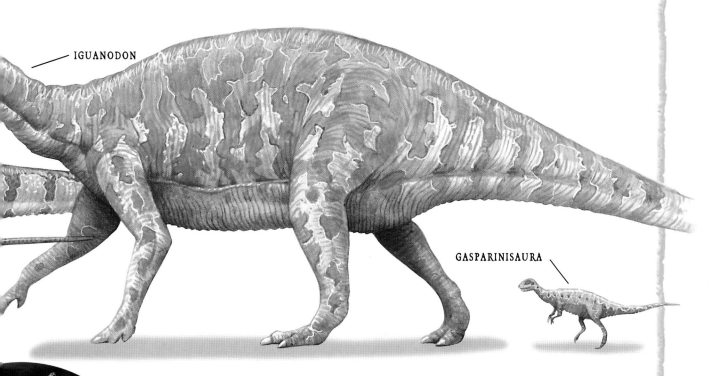

IGUANODON

GASPARINISAURA

MEET THE FAMILY

The modern view of *Iguanodon* is that it was too heavy to spend much time on its hind legs, so it moved on all fours. Since it was discovered, scientists have found many more iguanodontids. Australian *Muttaburrasaurus* was slightly smaller. American *Tenontosaurus* had a particularly long tail. The most primitive member of the group was *Gasparinisaura* from Argentina, the size of a turkey.

IGUANODON FOOD

Iguanodon lived in northern Europe during Early Cretaceous times. It wandered in herds across swampy landscapes, knee-deep in reed-beds of horsetail plants that grew just like our modern species. The herds probably grazed on these horsetails as they moved from one area to another.

TRIASSIC 248-206 MYA	EARLY/MID JURASSIC 206-159 MYA	LATE JURASSIC 159-144 MYA	EARLY CRETACEOUS 144-99 MYA	LATE CRETACEOUS 99-65 MYA

THE DUCKBILLS

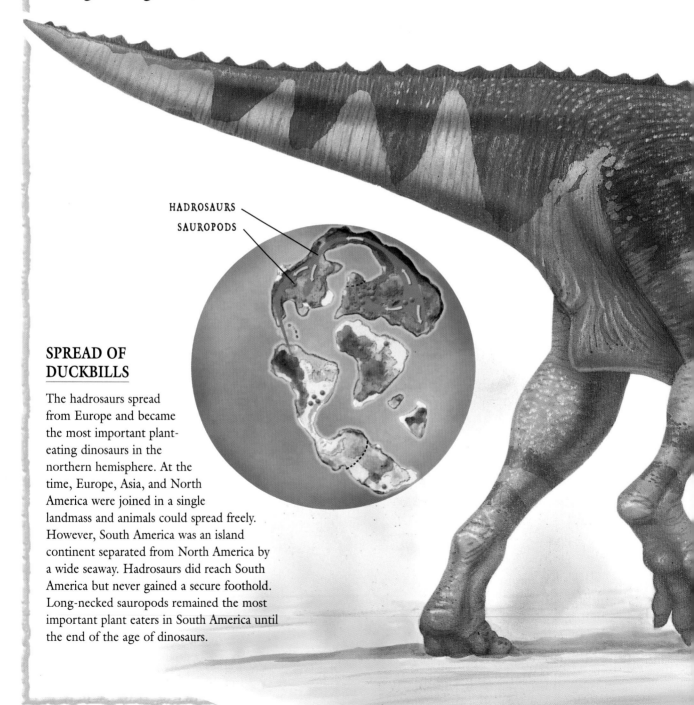

In the Late Cretaceous, a new group of ornithopods evolved from the iguanodontids. The vegetation was changing: primitive forests were giving way to modern-looking woodlands of oak, beech, and other broad-leaved trees with undergrowth of flowering herbs. These new dinosaurs, the hadrosaurs, spread and flourished in the forests throughout Europe, Asia, and North America. They had thousands of grinding teeth and a broad beak at the front of the mouth.

HADROSAURS

SAUROPODS

SPREAD OF DUCKBILLS

The hadrosaurs spread from Europe and became the most important plant-eating dinosaurs in the northern hemisphere. At the time, Europe, Asia, and North America were joined in a single landmass and animals could spread freely. However, South America was an island continent separated from North America by a wide seaway. Hadrosaurs did reach South America but never gained a secure foothold. Long-necked sauropods remained the most important plant eaters in South America until the end of the age of dinosaurs.

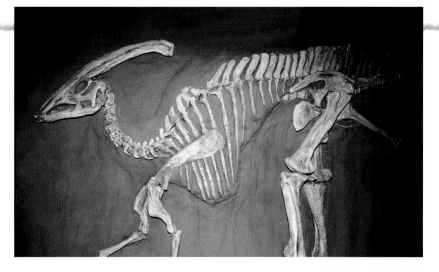

HEAD CRESTS

Some hadrosaurs, like this *Parasaurolophus*, had elaborate head crests. Mostly made of hollow bone connected to the nostrils, they were probably used for signaling one another through dense forests. Each type of hadrosaur had a unique crest shape to distinguish different herds from one another. Those with flat heads or solid crests probably supported an inflatable flap of skin that could have been puffed up like a frog's throat to make a noise.

MODERN CONIFERS

Modern conifers, such as pine and spruce, as well as the broad-leaved trees, such as oak and ash, appeared in Cretaceous times. Until then, the more primitive conifers, such as monkey puzzle trees, had sustained the sauropods. Hadrosaurs were well equipped for dealing with the new conifers. They used their broad beaks to scrape off the needles and their batteries of teeth to grind them down before swallowing.

HADROSAURUS

Hadrosaurus was, like *Iguanodon*, essentially a two-footed, plant-eating dinosaur which as an adult would have been rather too heavy to spend much time on its hind legs. It would have moved about on all fours, a theory confirmed by the fleshy, weight-bearing pads on its forelimbs. *Hadrosaurus'* tail was very deep and flat, which once led scientists to think the hadrosaur may have been a swimming animal — an idea that has now been discarded. Its most distinctive feature was its broad, flat, duck-like beak.

TRIASSIC 248-206 MYA	EARLY/MID JURASSIC 206-159 MYA	LATE JURASSIC 159-144 MYA	EARLY CRETACEOUS 144-99 MYA	LATE CRETACEOUS 99-65 MYA

DEATH OF DENVER STEGOSAURUS

A team from the Denver Museum discovered a *Stegosaurus* skeleton with a diseased tail after a broken tail spike became infected. The weakened animal then died during a drought. Its stomach bloated, rolling it over on its back. The drought ended and a nearby river burst its banks, covering the *Stegosaurus* with silt. All this was deduced 140 million years later from the fossil and the types of rocks found nearby. Such study of what leads to fossilization is known as *taphonomy*.

STEGOSAURUS

Stegosaurus lived in North America at the end of the Jurassic Period. A big four-footed animal up to 26 feet (8 m) long, with shorter legs at the front, a double row of plates along its back, and two pairs of spikes sticking out toward the tip of its tail, it had a small head and a kind of armored mesh protecting its throat. Some scientists believe the plates formed an armored shield. Others insist they acted as heat exchangers to cool its blood by turning the plates to the wind or to absorb warmth from the Sun.

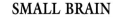

SMALL BRAIN

The head of a St*egosaurus* was quite small and held a very small brain. Like ornithopods, it had a beak at the front of its mouth and cheeks along the side.

TRIASSIC	EARLY/MID JURASSIC	LATE JURASSIC	EARLY CRETACEOUS	LATE CRETACEOUS
248-206 MYA	206-159 MYA	159-144 MYA	144-99 MYA	99-65 MYA

THE PLATED LIZARDS

Not long after ornithopods came into existence, all kinds of other dinosaurs began to evolve from them. Many sported armor of one kind or another. They were too heavy to spend much time on two legs and became mostly four-footed beasts. One group had armor arranged in a double row of plates or spikes down its back and tail. These plated dinosaurs were known as stegosaurs.

FLAT

PAIRS

SINGLE OVERLAPPING ROW

DOUBLE ALTERNATING

UNDER ATTACK

PLATE PUZZLES

The back plates of *Stegosaurus* were embedded in its skin but not attached directly to its skeleton. This has caused uncertainty about how they were arranged. One theory suggests that the plates lay flat as armor along the animal's back. Another is that they stood upright in pairs. Yet another says they had a single upright row of overlapping plates. The most widely accepted view is that they stood in a double row, alternating with one another. Some scientists suggest that the muscles at the base of the plates would have allowed *Stegosaurus* to point them at an attacker.

CLEVER TAIL

Most stegosaurids had two pairs of spikes at the end of their tail. The tails were usually quite flexible and could have been swung sideways with some force against the flanks of an attacker. In the hipbones was a gap that may have held a concentration of nerves to control the hind legs and tail and a gland that supplied extra energy. This space in the tail gave rise to a once-popular misconception that stegosaurids had two brains.

A WORLD OF STEGOSAURS

*S*tegosaurus was not the only stegosaurid. There were many others, ranging from North America through Europe to Asia. They probably evolved from an Early Jurassic group called the scelidosaurids. The most primitive of the stegosaurids we know were found in Middle Jurassic rocks in China. From such medium-sized animals developed a wide range of plated and spiked dinosaurs. By the Middle Cretaceous they had all but died out. The remains of a possible stegosaurid was found in Upper Cretaceous rocks in India. Perhaps the group lasted longer in India, an island continent at the time.

KENTROSAURUS ————————

EAST AFRICAN DISCOVERIES

The Humboldt Museum in Berlin has a collection of Late Jurassic dinosaurs excavated from East Africa in the 1920s. Among them are the stegosaurid *Kentrosaurus*, which was very similar to the North American *Stegosaurus*. There were also sauropods such as *Dicraeosaurus* (shown left), which was similar to *Diplodocus*.

AN EARLY STEGOSAURID

Cow-sized *Scelidosaurus*, known from the Lower Jurassic rocks of England, was a four-footed herbivore covered with small studs of armor. It may have been an ancestor of the stegosaurids or of the later Cretaceous nodosaurids of North America and the Middle Jurassic to Late Cretaceous ankylosaurids of Europe, North America, and Asia. It may even have been ancestral to both.

VARIETY OF STEGOSAURIDS

The most primitive stegosaurid known is the 13-foot- (4-m-) long *Huayangosaurus* from Middle Jurassic China. Later stegosaurids had shorter front legs, but the legs of *Huayangosaurus* hardly varied. Its armor included paired narrow back spikes and a tail with two pairs of spikes. It also had a pair of shoulder spikes, as did some later stegosaurids. *Dacenturus* (Late Jurassic Europe) had low, rounded plates on its shoulders and back and tall spikes down its tail. *Kentrosaurus* (Late Jurassic Africa) had its center of gravity at its hips, so, like some sauropods, it could rise on its hind legs to browse (as could *Stegosaurus*). *Wuerhosaurus* (Early Cretaceous China) was as big as *Stegosaurus* and had long low back plates.

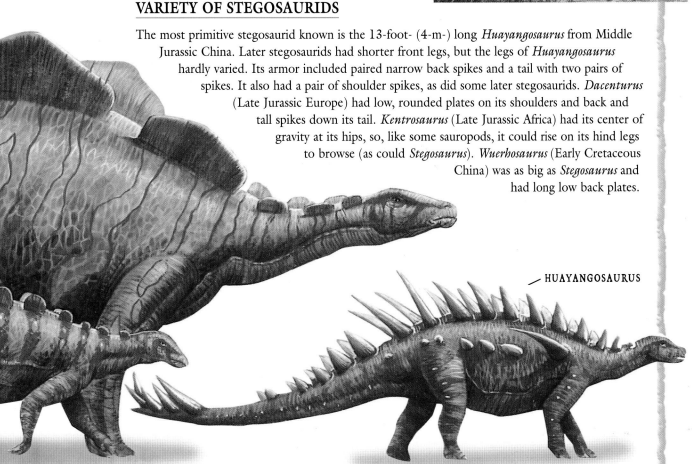

HUAYANGOSAURUS

TRIASSIC 248-206 MYA	EARLY/MID JURASSIC 206-159 MYA	LATE JURASSIC 159-144 MYA	EARLY CRETACEOUS 144-99 MYA	LATE CRETACEOUS 99-65 MYA

THE NODOSAURIDS - SPIKY DINOSAURS

GASTONIA

One of the best-preserved nodosaurid fossils ever found was *Gastonia*. Its armor formed a solid shield. Spikes stood up over the shoulders, and it had a series of broad, flat spines, almost blades, sticking outward and running down each side from the neck to the tip of the tail. It was found in Early Cretaceous rocks in Utah, but an almost identical Early Cretaceous dinosaur has been found in England.

As the Jurassic Period passed, the armored stegosaurids became extinct and other groups of armored dinosaurs evolved. The two most closely related groups were the nodosaurids and the ankylosaurids. Each had small, bony plates across their broad backs. These plates stretched up the neck to the head and down the tail and would have had horny covers that made the animal's back impregnable. The distinctive feature of the nodosaurid group was the presence of long, tough spikes sticking out sideways and upward from the shoulders and from the sides.

SPIKY CUSTOMERS

Two related groups of armored dinosaurs existed in Cretaceous times. The nodosaurids were characterized by spikes on the neck and sides, while the ankylosaurids had clubs on the ends of their tails.

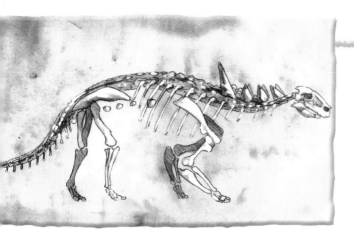

SAUROPELTA SKELETON

The solid back plate armor is the most commonly fossilized part of a nodosaurid and is usually found upside down. If a nodosaurid died and fell into a river, it may have been washed out to sea. As it decayed, expanding digestive gases in its gut would have turned it over, its heavy back acting as a keel. As it settled on the seabed, it would be buried and eventually fossilized in that position.

STRUTHIOSAURUS

Not all nodosaurids were big animals. *Struthiosaurus* from Upper Cretaceous rocks of central Europe was only 6.5 feet (2 m) long, with a body the size of a dog. It was probably an island dweller. Island animals, such as the modern Shetland pony, tend to evolve into smaller forms to make best use of limited food.

SAUROPELTA

One of the earliest nodosaurids was *Sauropelta* of Montana and Wyoming. It had an arched back, long tail, and longer hind legs. Like all other nodosaurids, its neck, back, and tail were covered with armor. *Sauropelta*'s long, defensive spines were confined to the neck and shoulders and spread outward and upward.

TRIASSIC 248-206 MYA	EARLY/MID JURASSIC 206-159 MYA	LATE JURASSIC 159-144 MYA	EARLY CRETACEOUS 144-99 MYA	LATE CRETACEOUS 99-65 MYA

EUOPLOCEPHALUS

The best known of the ankylosaurids is *Euoplocephalus*, 16 feet (5 m) long and living a little earlier than *Ankylosaurus* in Alberta, Canada. Its back was a mass of armor, the head an armored box. Even the eyelids were armored and slammed shut like the steel shutters of a battleship whenever danger approached. It used its powerful club tail to repel attack from even the most intimidating of predators, such as this *Tyrannosaurus*.

TAIL CLUB

The tail of *Euoplocephalus* and other ankylosaurids had a heavy club at the end. To support it, the vertebrae of half the tail were fused together in a solid bar, making it like the shaft of a medieval mace. The muscles at the broad hips and the flexible part of the base of the tail would have allowed this club to be swung sideways with great force against the legs and flanks of a raiding meat-eating dinosaur, breaking bones and disabling the attacker for life.

A HEARTY APPETITE

Without its shield of armor, *Euoplocephalus* was a heavy, four-footed animal. Its hips were broad, but the design allowed the intestines to be carried well back. The intestines would have been massive and probably contained fermenting chambers like those of modern cows.

ANKYLOSAURIDS - THE CLUB-TAILS

Ankylosaurids were closely related to nodosaurids but mostly came later, toward the end of the Cretaceous. With their armored necks and backs, they looked like their relatives, but instead of having spikes on the shoulders and sides, they had a heavy, bony club at the end of the tail. This could have been devastating when swung at an enemy. It may also have been used as a decoy. Perhaps it looked like a head on a neck, causing meat eaters to attack it instead of the more vulnerable front end.

CRETACEOUS UNDERGROWTH

By the end of the Cretaceous Period, modern plants had evolved. Beneath the broad-leaved trees was an undergrowth of flowering herbs such as buttercups. The ankylosaurids and the nodosaurids carried their heads low and their mouths close to the ground. They were evidently low-level feeders that ate the flowering herbs.

TRIASSIC 248-206 MYA	EARLY/MID JURASSIC 206-159 MYA	LATE JURASSIC 159-144 MYA	EARLY CRETACEOUS 144-99 MYA	LATE CRETACEOUS 99-65 MYA

HEADS

Each group of pachycephalosaurids had its own type of skull shape and ornamentation. *Stegoceras* and *Homalocephale*, from Mongolia, had sloping heads, higher at the rear, the latter with an elaborate head crest. *Prenocephale*, also from Mongolia, had a more rounded, dome-like head. Both had decorative lumps around the bony crown. North American *Stygimoloch* was perhaps the strangest, with a weird array of spikes and spines all around its dome. These were probably used for intimidation rather than fighting. All pachycephalosaurids lived in the Late Cretaceous Period.

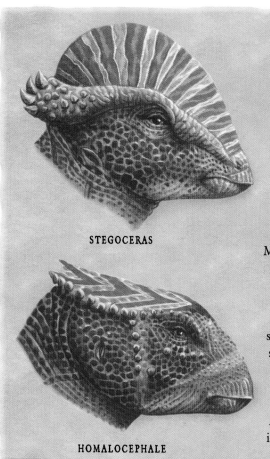

STEGOCERAS

HOMALOCEPHALE

STYGIMOLOCH

PRENOCEPHALE

MODERN SPARRERS

In the North American Rocky Mountains, modern bighorn sheep and mountain goats go through an annual ritual in which the males fight the flock leader to test his strength. The construction of their skulls and horns protects them from suffering much damage when they bash against one another. Pachycephalosaurids probably had similar rituals.

| TRIASSIC 248-206 MYA | EARLY/MID JURASSIC 206-159 MYA | LATE JURASSIC 159-144 MYA | EARLY CRETACEOUS 144-99 MYA | LATE CRETACEOUS 99-65 MYA |

BONEHEADS

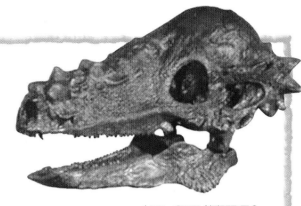

Imagine a dinosaur, a two-footed, plant-eating dinosaur such as an ornithopod, but give it a very high forehead so it looks brainy. What you would have is a pachycephalosaurid — another dinosaur group descended from the ornithopods. The intelligent look is actually false. The brain in that head is tiny, and the roof of the skull is made up of thick bone. We think the bone on top of the head was a weapon — a kind of battering ram. This was probably not for use against predators but for display in courtship battles.

ALL CREATURES GREAT AND SMALL

There was a great range of sizes in pachycephalosaurids. The largest known, at 16 feet (5 m) long, was North American *Pachycephalosaurus*. The smallest was *Micropachycephalosaurus* from China, which was about the size of a rabbit. This very small dinosaur has the longest dinosaur name ever given.

HORNED BATTLERS

Stegoceras is the most complete known pachycephalosaurid. Its head bone and strong neck provided great protection. They seem to have lived in herds. The males probably fought each other to lead the herd; the strongest would mate with the females.

HARD HEADS

Dinosaur skulls are rarely preserved as fossils, but pachycephalosaurid skulls were different. The top bone of the skull was so massive it often survived as a fossil. Commonly the only part of the animal preserved, these skulls are often found very battered. This suggests they were washed down a river for long distances before being buried in sediment. This may mean that these were mountain-living animals.

61

THE PRIMITIVE-HORNED DINOSAURS

The last of the plant-eating dinosaur groups existed from the mid to Late Cretaceous. Like the ankylosaurids and the nodosaurids, they lived in North America and in Asia, and they also evolved from ornithopods. They were equipped with armor, but it was confined solely to the head. Early types were lightly built and very ornithopod-like, but in later forms the armor on the head became so heavy that they moved around as four-footed animals. Flamboyant neck shields and horns evolved, and these horned dinosaurs became known as the ceratopsians.

AN EARLY SHEEP

Scientists regard *Protoceratops* as the sheep of Late Cretaceous Mongolia. Similar in size to sheep, they lived in herds and grazed the sparse vegetation of the arid landscape. One particular skeleton was found with the skeleton of a fierce carnivore, *Velociraptor*, clinging to its head shield. The meat eater had attacked the ceratopsian with its killing claws, but the ceratopsian must have fought back with its big beak; both dinosaurs lost their lives during the fight.

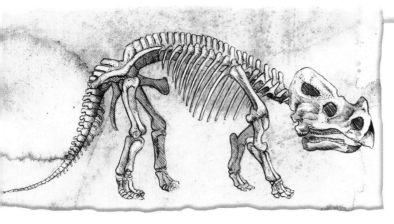

BIG BROTHER

By the time *Montanoceratops* had evolved, toward the end of the Late Cretaceous, ceratopsians were bigger and had developed horns. *Montanoceratops* was about 10 feet (3 m) long and walked on all fours. Like its two-footed ancestors, however, it had claws on its feet. In later ceratopsians, the toenails developed into hooves, which were better able to carry the weight of big animals.

ARCHAEOCERATOPS

The most primitive of the ceratopsians known is *Archaeoceratops*. It was a very small animal, about 3 feet (1 m) long, and scampered nimbly on hind legs on the plains of Early Cretaceous China. It had a head that was very similar to that of *Psittacosaurus*. Its skeleton was so primitive and generalized it is possible that its descendants gave rise to the big ceratopsians that were to follow.

WHO'S A PRETTY BOY?

An early relative of the ceratopsians was the 5-foot- (1.5-m-) long parrot-lizard *Psittacosaurus*. It developed a very strong beak and powerful jaws for plucking and chopping the tough vegetation it ate. A bony ridge around the back of the skull anchored its strong jaw muscles. The bony ridge and its big beak gave the skull a square shape, and the head must have looked a bit like the big-beaked head of a modern parrot.

CYCAD FOSSIL

At the end of the Cretaceous Period, the old-style vegetation was largely replaced by modern species of plants. However, some of the older types of palmlike cycads remained in some regions. In the areas where they occurred, the ceratopsians may have relied on these plants. Their narrow beaks could have reached into the palmlike clump of fronds and selected the best pieces, and their strong jaws could have shredded the tough leaves.

TRIASSIC 248-206 MYA	EARLY/MID JURASSIC 206-159 MYA	LATE JURASSIC 159-144 MYA	EARLY CRETACEOUS 144-99 MYA	LATE CRETACEOUS 99-65 MYA

VARIETY OF HEADS

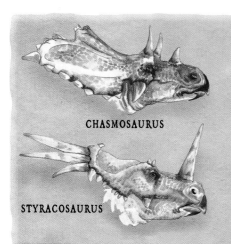

CHASMOSAURUS

STYRACOSAURUS

Ceratopsians all had the same body shape, but their different shapes of shield and horn arrangements made each type easily recognizable to its own herd. *Styracosaurus* had a monumental horn on its nose and an array of horns around its shield. *Chasmosaurus* had an enormous, sail-like shield. *Einiosaurus* had a long nose horn that curved forward and a pair of straight horns at the edge of its shield. *Acheluosaurus* had a battering ram on its nose, a pair of short, bladelike horns above its eyes, and a curved pair at the shield-edge.

ALL FOR ONE

The horns of ceratopsians would have been used to defend themselves and their herd against big carnivores and also to tussle with one another over position in the herd. Having locked horns, they would have pushed and shoved until one of them gave way. Little harm would have come to the loser. While traveling, the ceratopsians may have kept their young at the center of the herd to protect them. If attacked by carnivores, they may have formed a circle with the youngsters in the center and the adults facing outward so that the attackers were faced with the shields and horns of all the herd. Today, musk oxen protect their herd this way.

WILDEBEEST

We know ceratopsians moved in herds because we have found bone beds consisting of many hundreds, even thousands, of skeletons. The animals would have been migrating, traveling in herds to areas where there was more food at a particular time of year. When crossing a river, they may have been caught by a sudden flash flood that washed them away and dumped their bodies. This still happens in Africa today as herds of wildebeest migrate from one feeding ground to another.

THE BIG-HORNED DINOSAURS

The big ceratopsians were probably the most spectacular Late Cretaceous dinosaurs. They were all four-footed and mostly as big as today's rhinoceros. The ridge of bone around the neck had evolved into a broad shield. They also had an array of long horns on the face. The skulls of the big ceratopsians were so tough that many were preserved as fossils. There were two main lines of evolution. One group developed long frills and a pair of long horns above the eyes; the other had shorter frills and tended to have a single horn on the nose.

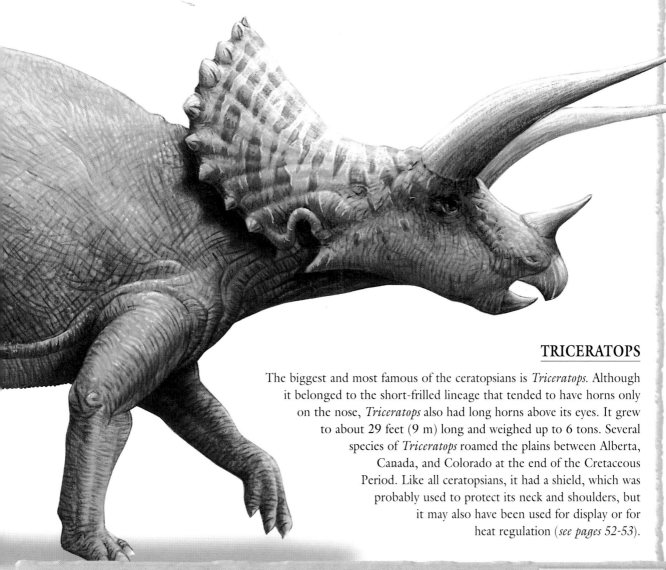

TRICERATOPS

The biggest and most famous of the ceratopsians is *Triceratops*. Although it belonged to the short-frilled lineage that tended to have horns only on the nose, *Triceratops* also had long horns above its eyes. It grew to about 29 feet (9 m) long and weighed up to 6 tons. Several species of *Triceratops* roamed the plains between Alberta, Canada, and Colorado at the end of the Cretaceous Period. Like all ceratopsians, it had a shield, which was probably used to protect its neck and shoulders, but it may also have been used for display or for heat regulation (*see pages 52-53*).

TRIASSIC 248-206 MYA	EARLY/MID JURASSIC 206-159 MYA	LATE JURASSIC 159-144 MYA	EARLY CRETACEOUS 144-99 MYA	LATE CRETACEOUS 99-65 MYA

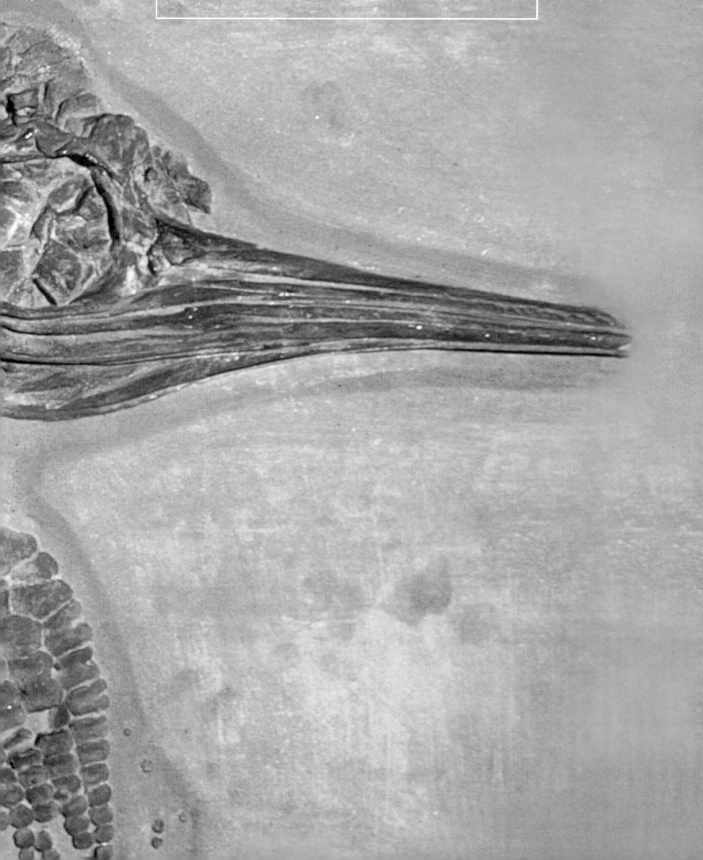

IN THE SEA

A RETRO-PIONEER

Spinoaequalis, the earliest-known land animal to return to a water-living existence, was a lizardlike beast found in Upper Carboniferous marine sediments in Kansas. Its name means "equal spine," which refers to the strong spines on the tail that made a flat vertical paddle to which strong muscles were attached. This is the tail of a swimming animal. The rest of the skeleton is that of a land-living creature.

A FRESHWATER PUZZLE

Mesosaurus was a freshwater reptile, about 3 feet (1 meter) long, with a flattened swimming tail and powerful webbed hind legs. It probably used its tail and hind legs to drive itself through the water and steered and stabilized itself with its webbed front feet. Its teeth were fine and needle-like and were probably used for filtering invertebrates from the water to eat. The odd thing about it, though, is the fact that its skeletons are found in Lower Permian rocks in both South Africa and Brazil. Scientists wondered how the remains of a freshwater animal were fossilized on two widely separated continents. It was the first piece of evidence in support of a revolutionary concept called "plate tectonics."

ABOUT PLATE TECTONICS

In Permian times, when *Mesosaurus* was alive, there was no Atlantic Ocean. What is now Africa and South America were part of a single vast landmass called Pangaea. The same kinds of animals lived all over the world because there were no oceans to separate them. The presence of the skeleton of *Mesosaurus* in South Africa and Brazil was one of the first pieces of evidence supporting the theory of continental drift — now better known as "plate tectonics."

THE FIRST SWIMMERS

All life came from the sea. Scientists estimate that life appeared 3.5 billion years ago and that plants and animals only relatively recently came out on to land (about 400 million years ago for plants and 300 million years ago for animals). Some of the first land creatures evolved into reptiles and dinosaurs. But the ways of evolution are complex. Almost as soon as life on land was established, some life forms returned to the sea to exploit new food sources. As early as 250 million years ago, water-living animals had evidently evolved from land-living ancestors.

A MODERN EXAMPLE

The Galapagos marine iguana, which looks and lives very much like some of the early swimming reptiles, has adopted a partially aquatic way of life because it feeds on seaweed. Its lizard body, legs, and feet show that it is a land-living animal, but its muscular, flexible tail is ideal for swimming. It also can hold its breath for long periods, and it can remove from its system excess salt absorbed from seawater. These are adaptations that fail to show up on fossil animals, so we do not know if early swimming reptiles had them.

THE BUOYANCY PROBLEM

Hovasaurus, from Upper Permian rocks found in Madagascar, had a swimming tail twice the length of its body. Although this tail was so long that it would have been difficult to use on land, its feet were those of a land-living reptile. Most skeletons of *Hovasaurus* have pebbles in the stomach area. Evidently *Hovasaurus* swallowed stones to adjust its buoyancy underwater. This swimming technique was used by animals whose ancestors were land-living animals (*see page 76*).

PERMIAN 354–290 MYA	CARBONIFEROUS 290–248 MYA	TRIASSIC 248–206 MYA	EARLY/MID JURASSIC 206–159 MYA	LATE JURASSIC 159–146 MYA

LIFE AFTER DEATH

The science of taphonomy deals with what happens to an animal after it dies and how it becomes a fossil. Here is how this process occurs at sea.

1. When an animal dies, it may float on the surface for a while until the gases generated in its decaying tissues disperse.

2. Eventually, it sinks to the bottom of the sea. A less buoyant animal may go straight to the bottom. There it may be scavenged by bottom-living creatures, its parts broken up and dispersed.

3. If sand and mud are being deposited rapidly on the seabed, the body is quickly buried before too much damage is done.

4. After millions of years, the sand and mud will be compressed and cemented together as rock, and the bones of the dead animal will have been replaced by minerals. It will have become a fossil.

A MODERN TURTLE

The turtle is a slow-moving aquatic reptile that is shelled above and below. Its paddle limbs allow it to move through the water with a flying action. Protected from its enemies and surrounded by sources of food, it does not need speed or a streamlined shape to thrive.

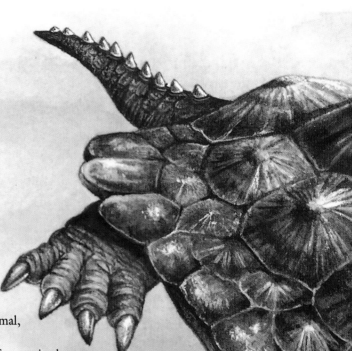

AN EARLY WINNER

A broad body shape works well for a slow-moving animal, but such a creature remains vulnerable to attack from predators. This threat encouraged the development of armor in the reptiles that we know today as turtles. The earliest turtle, *Proganochelys*, dates from the Late Triassic and lived in Germany. Its body shape and the arrangement of its shell are very similar to the modern turtle, which has not changed much in 215 million years.

BIG IS BEAUTIFUL

The biggest turtle known, *Archelon*, cruised the inland sea that covered much of North America in Late Cretaceous times. At almost 13 feet (4 meters) long, it was bigger than a rowboat. Its shell was a system of bony struts covered by tough skin, much like the skin of the biggest of the modern turtles, the leatherback. It probably fed on soft things, such as jellyfish, and like the modern leatherback, its jaws were not very strong.

A SCHOOL OF SWIMMING REPTILES

We have a good record of water-living animals because, in an environment where sediment constantly accumulates, these creatures have a better chance of becoming fossilized. From these fossils, we know that many sea creatures were in fact reptiles that left dry land for a new life in the water. With more food in the water than on land and fewer predators in the sea, an aquatic life would have been appealing. Reptiles can adapt easily to such a lifestyle. They have a low metabolic rate and can cope without oxygen for some time. In addition, moving around in water takes only about a quarter of the energy of moving around on land.

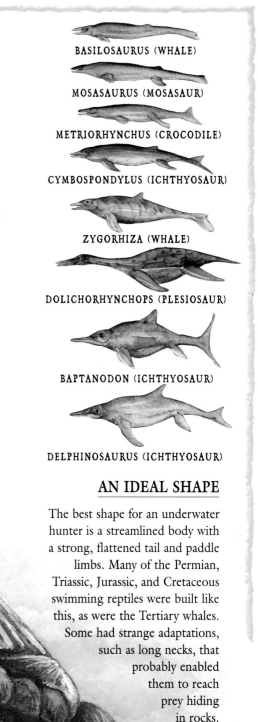

BASILOSAURUS (WHALE)

MOSASAURUS (MOSASAUR)

METRIORHYNCHUS (CROCODILE)

CYMBOSPONDYLUS (ICHTHYOSAUR)

ZYGORHIZA (WHALE)

DOLICHORHYNCHOPS (PLESIOSAUR)

BAPTANODON (ICHTHYOSAUR)

DELPHINOSAURUS (ICHTHYOSAUR)

AN IDEAL SHAPE

The best shape for an underwater hunter is a streamlined body with a strong, flattened tail and paddle limbs. Many of the Permian, Triassic, Jurassic, and Cretaceous swimming reptiles were built like this, as were the Tertiary whales. Some had strange adaptations, such as long necks, that probably enabled them to reach prey hiding in rocks.

TRIASSIC 248-206 MYA	EARLY/MID JURASSIC 206-159 MYA	LATE JURASSIC 159-144 MYA	EARLY CRETACEOUS 144-97 MYA	LATE CRETACEOUS 97-65 MYA

PLACODONTS - THE SHELL-SEEKERS

PLACODUS

The most typical of the placodonts was *Placodus* itself. In appearance it looked somewhat like an enormous newt, about 7 feet (2 m) long, with a chunky body, a paddle-shaped tail, webbed feet, and a short head.

Water-living animals may have evolved from land-living animals for a variety of reasons. Most persuasive of these is the idea that when a good food supply exists, nature will develop something to exploit it. Shellfish represent one such food supply. The earliest reptiles that seemed to be well adapted to feeding on shellfish were the placodonts. Although they still needed to come to the surface to breathe, they rooted on the bed of the Tethys Ocean that spread across southern Europe in Triassic times.

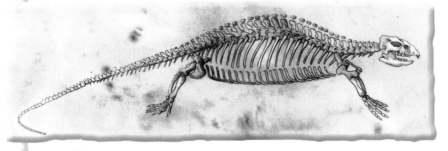

BUILT FOR BUOYANCY

A glimpse of the skeleton of *Placodus* reveals one of its main adaptations to an underwater way of life — "pachystosis." This means that its bones were broad and heavy, perfect for feeding on the bottom of the ocean. Animals that have pachystosis also have big lungs to help regulate buoyancy. To accommodate its huge lungs, *Placodus* developed a broad rib cage. A modern animal with these adaptations is the sea otter. Its weight and large lung capacity enable it to walk along the seabed with ease, hunting shellfish. *Placodus* would have done the same.

TRIASSIC 248-206 MYA	EARLY/MID JURASSIC 206-159 MYA	LATE JURASSIC 159-144 MYA	EARLY CRETACEOUS 144-97 MYA	LATE CRETACEOUS 97-65 MYA

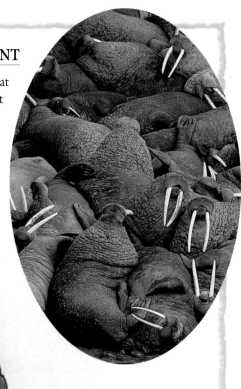

The walrus is a modern sea animal that subsists on shellfish. Its two great tusks are used for prying shellfish from rocks, and it has crushing teeth at the back of its mouth. The tusks are also used as ice picks and for mating displays. We do not know if the protruding teeth of the placodonts had similar functions.

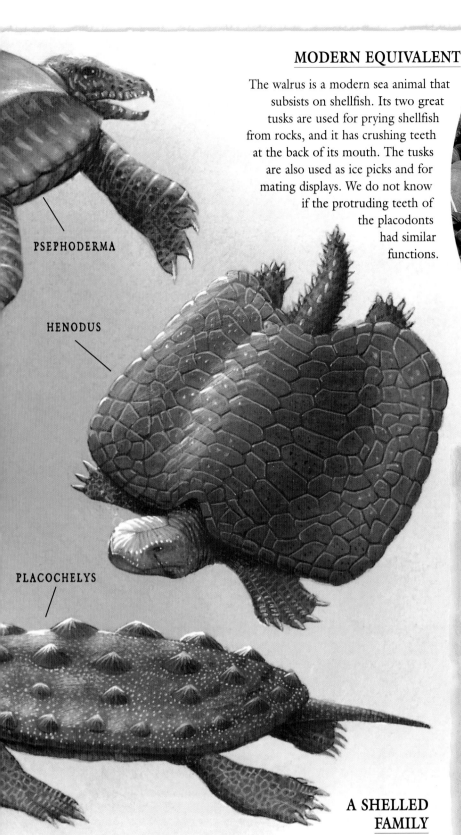

PSEPHODERMA

HENODUS

PLACOCHELYS

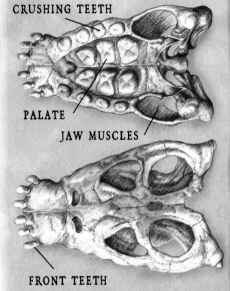

CRUSHING TEETH

PALATE

JAW MUSCLES

FRONT TEETH

POWERFUL BITE

From below, the protruding front teeth of *Placodus* are obvious. These prominent teeth were used for plucking shells from the rocks and the seafloor. Further back, the jaws have strong crushing teeth, and even the palate is paved with broad, flat teeth, all ideal for smashing the shells of shellfish. Holes in the side of the skull show where very powerful jaw muscles were attached. *Placodus* would have eaten brachiopods as well as bivalves similar to those that survive today.

A SHELLED FAMILY

Because they were slow-moving animals, the placodonts must have been vulnerable to the meat eaters of the time. Many developed shells on their backs as protection. In some types, the shells were extensive and looked much like those of turtles, but the two groups of animals were not related. The similar shells developed independently among animals with the same lifestyle in the same environment — a process known as "convergent evolution."

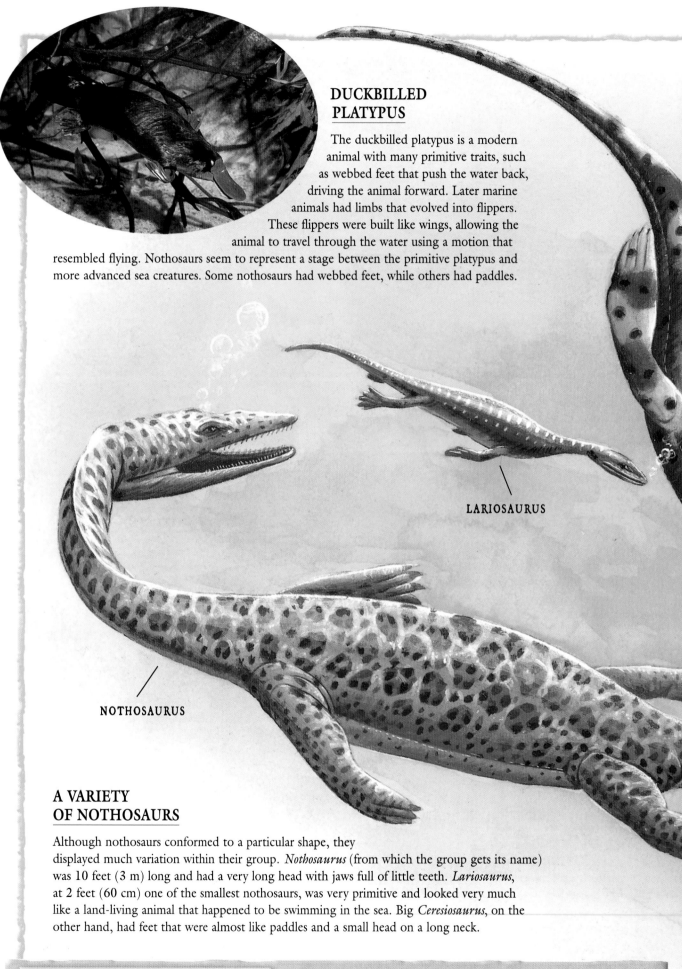

DUCKBILLED PLATYPUS

The duckbilled platypus is a modern animal with many primitive traits, such as webbed feet that push the water back, driving the animal forward. Later marine animals had limbs that evolved into flippers. These flippers were built like wings, allowing the animal to travel through the water using a motion that resembled flying. Nothosaurs seem to represent a stage between the primitive platypus and more advanced sea creatures. Some nothosaurs had webbed feet, while others had paddles.

LARIOSAURUS

NOTHOSAURUS

A VARIETY OF NOTHOSAURS

Although nothosaurs conformed to a particular shape, they displayed much variation within their group. *Nothosaurus* (from which the group gets its name) was 10 feet (3 m) long and had a very long head with jaws full of little teeth. *Lariosaurus*, at 2 feet (60 cm) one of the smallest nothosaurs, was very primitive and looked very much like a land-living animal that happened to be swimming in the sea. Big *Ceresiosaurus*, on the other hand, had feet that were almost like paddles and a small head on a long neck.

TRIASSIC 248-206 MYA	EARLY/MID JURASSIC 206-159 MYA	LATE JURASSIC 159-144 MYA	EARLY CRETACEOUS 144-97 MYA	LATE CRETACEOUS 97-65 MYA

BETWEEN THE LAND & THE SEA

The nothosaurs preceded the plesiosaurs, rulers of the Late Jurassic and Cretaceous seas. Like the placodonts, they are known mostly from sediments laid down in the Tethys Ocean, an ancient ocean that lay between Africa and Europe. Their necks, bodies, and tails were long, and they had webbed feet (although they could walk on land). Their hind limbs were much larger than their front limbs and were used mostly for swimming. They had many small, pointed teeth in long, narrow jaws for catching fish. Nothosaurs seem to represent a stage between land-living animals and fish-eating, seagoing animals like the plesiosaurs.

LET'S GO FISHING

The long jaws and sharp teeth of *Nothosaurus* were ideal for catching fish. The long neck would have been able to reach fast-swimming fish quickly, and the little teeth would have held the slippery prey firmly. These teeth can be seen in such modern fish-eating animals as crocodiles.

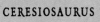

CERESIOSAURUS

NOTHOSAUR FOSSIL

Nothosaur fossils have been found in the Alps and in China. Although these animals had legs and toes, their limb bones were not strongly joined to one another and the hips and shoulders were quite weak. This weakened state shows that they were not well adapted to moving on land and were better at swimming than at walking.

STOMACH STONES

Most good fossilized skeletons of pliosaurs contain collections of gastroliths (stomach stones). Sea-living animals swallow stones to help adjust their ballast (weight). For animals that swim fast to catch their prey, this method is a more versatile system than building up the weight of the skeleton through pachystosis, a method adopted by the placodonts (*see page 72*).

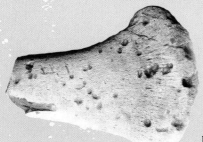

PLIOSAUR TOOTH MARKS

The limb bones of an elasmosaur found in Late Jurassic marine rocks in Dorset, England, have given scientists a dramatic clue to the feeding habits of the pliosaurs. Tooth marks punched deep into the bones match the set of teeth of a big pliosaur. Until this discovery, scientists thought that pliosaurs ate only fish and squid.

UNDERWATER ATTACK

From this evidence, we can build up a picture of a Late Jurassic marine incident. A long-necked elasmosaur feeds near the surface. A pliosaur cruises at some depth below, hunting fish and squid. By tasting the water, it knows the elasmosaur is nearby. Vomiting out a few stomach stones, it adjusts its buoyancy to allow it to rise. Then, when its prey is in view, the pliosaur "flies" toward the elasmosaur with strong thrusts of its flippers, closing in on a paddle and ripping it apart with its teeth.

| TRIASSIC 248-206 MYA | EARLY/MID JURASSIC 206-159 MYA | LATE JURASSIC 159-144 MYA | EARLY CRETACEOUS 144-97 MYA | LATE CRETACEOUS 97-65 MYA |

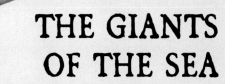

THE GIANTS OF THE SEA

The plesiosaurs were perhaps the most varied group of swimming reptiles during the time of the dinosaurs. They were ocean-going fish eaters, ranging in size from the length of a small seal to that of a medium-sized whale. They had broad bodies, short tails, and two pairs of winglike paddles with which they "flew" through ocean waters. One group had short necks and long heads; the other had long necks and very small heads (*see pages 78–81*). The short-necked types are called pliosaurs, and the long-necked types are elasmosaurs.

IN FOR THE KILL

Broad flanges at the back of the skull of a pliosaur must have held massive neck muscles, suggesting that pliosaurs grabbed their larger prey and pulled it to bits with a twisting action. Crocodiles in deep water dismember their food in exactly this way today.

BIG MOUTH

The most amazing feature of a pliosaur skeleton is its huge skull. The long jaws were equipped with many sharp teeth that were ideal for catching big fish and squid and also for seizing larger prey. The nostrils are surprisingly small and would not have been used for breathing. Instead, they would have been used for tasting the water and for judging the speed at which the animal was swimming. A pliosaur probably breathed through its mouth when it came to the surface.

LIOPLEURODON VERTEBRA

This is a vertebra from *Liopleurodon*, which existed in northern European waters at the end of the Jurassic Period. Pliosaurs were a wide-ranging group, with very similar animals existing in Europe at one time and on the other side of the world in Australia 80 million years later. It was probably *Liopleurodon* that attacked the elasmosaur in the incident described on page 76.

A RANGE OF PLIOSAURS

We used to think that pliosaurs were the biggest sea reptiles of all time. Now, however, we are finding the remains of beasts that were even bigger (*see page 87*). Nevertheless, the biggest pliosaurs were very big animals.

Many smaller pliosaurs also cruised the seas. Their different sizes and head shapes reflected their different lifestyles and the different foods they were eating. Some must have lived like penguins, darting and snatching at the weaving and dispersing schools of fish, but the biggest must have been the dolphins and toothed whales of their time. Often, all we know of a particular pliosaur is the skull. Using the skull as a guide and building models based on an agreed-upon plan, scientists have assumed that we can know what the rest of the body was like. Who knows for sure if they are right?

MONSTER OF THE DEEP

We used to think that the skull of the pliosaur *Kronosaurus* represented less than a quarter of the length of the whole animal, giving *Kronosaurus* a total length of 40–46 feet (12–14 m) — greater than the contemporary *Tyrannosaurus* on land. More recent studies suggest that the skull was about a third of the total length, making it 26 feet (8 m) long. That's still quite a monster!

TRIASSIC 248-206 MYA	EARLY/MID JURASSIC 206-159 MYA	LATE JURASSIC 159-144 MYA	EARLY CRETACEOUS 144-97 MYA	LATE CRETACEOUS 97-65 MYA

A HALFWAY STAGE

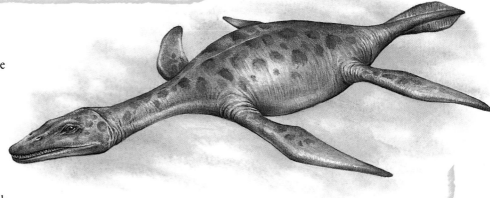

Fossilized bones of sea animals are much more common than those of land animals. They are often found on beaches, where the sea is eroding cliffs made of rock from the Mesozoic Era (which included the Triassic, Jurassic, and Cretaceous periods), or in quarries where rock from the same era is being extracted. One of the most complete plesiosaur skeletons ever found was 16 feet (5 m) long. *Rhomaleosaurus* was uncovered in 1851 from stone quarries in Barrow upon Soar, Leicestershire, central England. It featured widely spread ribs, and it has become the mascot of the village. Scientifically, the odd thing about *Rhomaleosaurus* is the fact that it has a long neck as well as a fairly large head. It is classed as a pliosaur, but it seems to represent a stage between the short-necked pliosaurs and the long-necked elasmosaurs.

SUPER-PENGUINS

Dolichorhynchops was a much smaller pliosaur, about 10 feet (3 m) long. It lived in the seas that covered Late Cretaceous Manitoba in Canada. Judging the animal by its build and its teeth, scientists feel that it swam easily among schools of fish that frequented the waters, snapping them up in its long, narrow jaws. It swam like modern penguins, using paddles to get around.

UNDERWATER FLIGHT

The plesiosaur paddle worked like a wing. Among the pliosaurs, the strongest muscles pushed the paddles forward, providing the animal with its power stroke. Among the elasmosaurs, there was as much muscle to pull the paddle back as to push it forward, allowing the body to turn very quickly and suggesting that the elasmosaurs had much more maneuverability than pliosaurs. Today, penguins use the same kind of swimming action.

"NESSIE"

For hundreds of years, many people have reported sightings of an elasmosaur-like creature in Loch Ness, in the Highlands of Scotland. This convincing picture was taken in 1977. But is it a dinosaur's head or a branch?

ARTISTIC IMPRESSIONS

Because of numerous fossil finds, the remains of plesiosaurs were known to fossil collectors for a long time before dinosaurs were discovered. This 19th-century engraving of a prehistoric coastal scene depicts a giant ichthyosaur being attacked by two long-necked plesiosaurs. Although far from perfect, depictions of sea creatures were much more accurate than those of the land-living dinosaurs from the same period.

ELASMOSAURS - THE LONG-NECKS

One early researcher described the long-necked plesiosaurs as "snakes threaded through turtles." The broad body and the winglike flippers are reminiscent of the ocean-going turtle, but the long neck and the little head full of vicious, pointed teeth are very different from those of the placid, grazing, shelled reptile we know today. Elasmosaurs were the sea serpents of their time. They existed alongside the pliosaurs in the oceans of the Jurassic and Cretaceous periods.

FLEXIBILITY

The great length of the elasmosaur neck, with its huge number of vertebrae, has led some to suggest that it would have been as flexible as a snake. But looking at the way the vertebrae are articulated, we can see that this was not quite true. From side to side the neck had a good degree of movement, but the neck was restricted in the up-and-down plane. Although an elasmosaur could reach downward with ease, it could not hold its head up like a swan on the surface.

CRYPTOCLIDUS

Cryptoclidus was a common elasmosaur found in Late Jurassic rocks of Europe. Its mounted skeleton can be seen in several museums. It is typical of the whole elasmosaur group, with its broad body with ribs above and below, the long neck, the mouthful of sharp, outward-pointing teeth, and the paddles made of packed bone.

TRIASSIC 248-206 MYA	EARLY/MID JURASSIC 206-159 MYA	LATE JURASSIC 159-144 MYA	EARLY CRETACEOUS 144-97 MYA	LATE CRETACEOUS 97-65 MYA

ELASMOSAUR LIFESTYLE

Elasmosaurs came in all sizes. As time went by, the group displayed a tendency to develop longer and longer necks. They may have hunted by ambush. The big body was probably used to disturb schools of fish, while the little head at the end of the long neck darted quickly into the group and speared individual fish on the long teeth. Moving the paddles in different directions would have turned the body very quickly in any direction. Their agility meant that elasmosaurs probably hunted on the surface, as opposed to the pliosaurs, who were built for sustained cruising at great depths.

ELASMOSAURUS

We take the name of the elasmosaur group from Late Cretaceous *Elasmosaurus*. This creature had the longest neck, in proportion to the body, of any animal known. It had 71 vertebrae, in contrast to the 28 or so of the earlier elasmosaurs. The neck took up more than half the length of the entire animal.

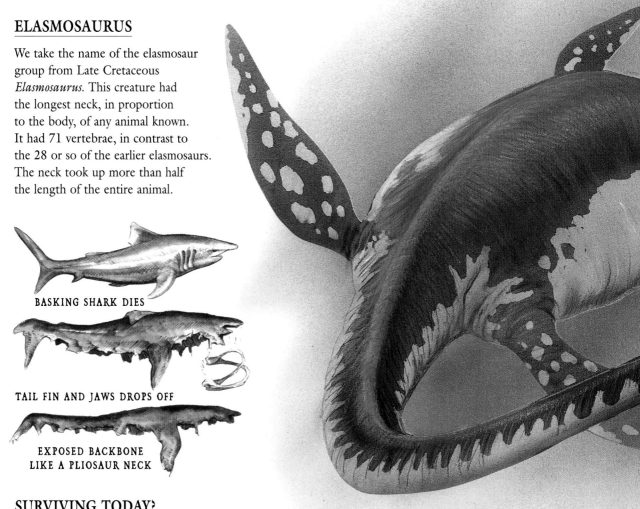

BASKING SHARK DIES

TAIL FIN AND JAWS DROPS OFF

EXPOSED BACKBONE
LIKE A PLIOSAUR NECK

SURVIVING TODAY?

Now and then we hear stories of people sighting sea serpents that have a distinct similarity to plesiosaurs. Several photographs exist of rotting carcasses with a plesiosaur look to them. The carcasses usually turn out to be those of basking sharks. Although a basking shark looks nothing like a plesiosaur in life, its dead body deteriorates in a particular pattern. The dorsal fin and the tail fin fall off, losing the shark's distinctive profile. Then the massive jaws drop away. This leaves a tiny brain case at the end of a long string of vertebrae. Instant plesiosaur!

TRIASSIC 248-206 MYA	EARLY/MID JURASSIC 206-159 MYA	LATE JURASSIC 159-144 MYA	EARLY CRETACEOUS 144-97 MYA	LATE CRETACEOUS 97-65 MYA

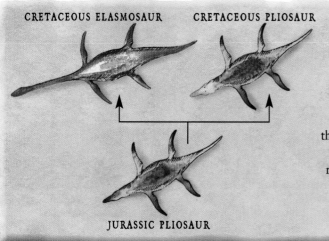

CRETACEOUS ELASMOSAUR   CRETACEOUS PLIOSAUR

JURASSIC PLIOSAUR

THE "POLYPHYLETIC" THEORY

It is possible that elasmosaurs were "polyphyletic," which means they did not evolve from one ancestor. The Jurassic elasmosaurs evolved from the same ancestors as the nothosaurs of the Triassic Period. However, the arrangement of the skull bones of the Cretaceous elasmosaurs has led some scientists to suggest that these later ones actually evolved from the short-necked pliosaurs of the Jurassic Period. The long neck developed independently in response to environmental pressures; there was food to be had for long-necked animals, so long-necked animals evolved. Most scientists, however, believe that all the elasmosaurs evolved from the same ancestors — that is, they were "monophyletic."

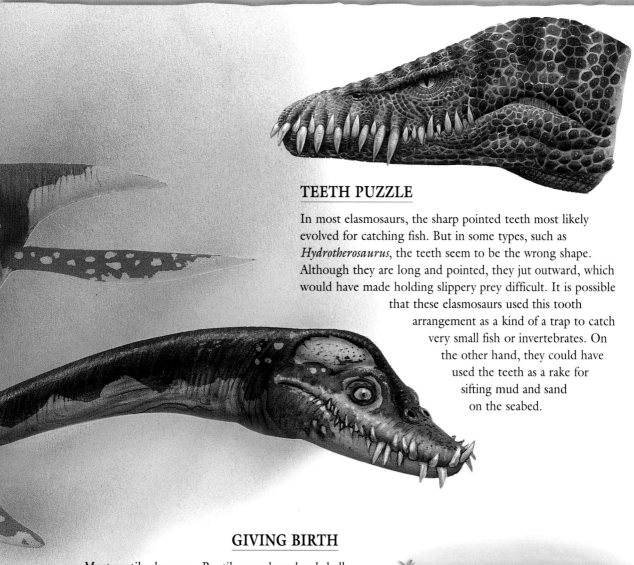

TEETH PUZZLE

In most elasmosaurs, the sharp pointed teeth most likely evolved for catching fish. But in some types, such as *Hydrotherosaurus*, the teeth seem to be the wrong shape. Although they are long and pointed, they jut outward, which would have made holding slippery prey difficult. It is possible that these elasmosaurs used this tooth arrangement as a kind of a trap to catch very small fish or invertebrates. On the other hand, they could have used the teeth as a rake for sifting mud and sand on the seabed.

GIVING BIRTH

Most reptiles lay eggs. Reptile eggs have hard shells through which the developing embryo can breathe. Unfortunately, reptiles thus cannot lay their eggs at sea, because the young would drown. It is possible that elasmosaurs laid eggs the way modern turtles do. This would mean that they came ashore at certain times of the year and scooped out a hole in the beach with their flippers. This process is a great effort for a modern turtle. Just imagine the effort for a 39-foot (12-m) plesiosaur!

A CLEAR IMAGE

Thinly layered, Late-Jurassic rocks at
Holzmaden in Germany are so fine
that they contain the impressions of
the softest organisms that lived and
died there. The bottom of the sea
(where the rocks formed) was so stagnant that nothing
lived — not even the bacteria that normally break down
once-living matter. Among the spectacular fossils found
there are the ichthyosaurs, with impressions of their soft
anatomy still preserved. Flesh and skin still exist as a fine
film of the original carbon. With this find, scientists were
able to determine for the first time that ichthyosaurs had
a dorsal fin and a big, fishlike fin on the tail.

A MODERN RENDERING

Now we can paint an accurate picture of what an ichthyosaur
looked like in life. From all the fossils we have found we
know that they had streamlined, dolphinlike bodies, with
fins on the back and tail. Unlike dolphins, the tail fin
was vertical, not horizontal. The ichthyosaur had two
pairs of paddles, the front pair usually bigger than
the hind pair.

AN ICHTHYOSAUR PIONEER

As with the plesiosaurs, the ichthyosaurs were known before the dinosaurs.
Early naturalists, who discovered them in eroding cliffs along the Dorset
coast in southern England, took them for the remains of ancient crocodiles.
Indeed, their long jaws and sharp teeth are very reminiscent of crocodiles.
Mary Anning (1799–1847), a professional fossil collector and dealer from
Lyme Regis in Dorset, is credited with finding the first complete fossil
ichthyosaur when she was 12 years old. This is a myth, but her collecting
and her dealings with the scientists of the day were crucial in furthering our
knowledge of these creatures.

ICHTHYOSAURS - THE FISH LIZARDS

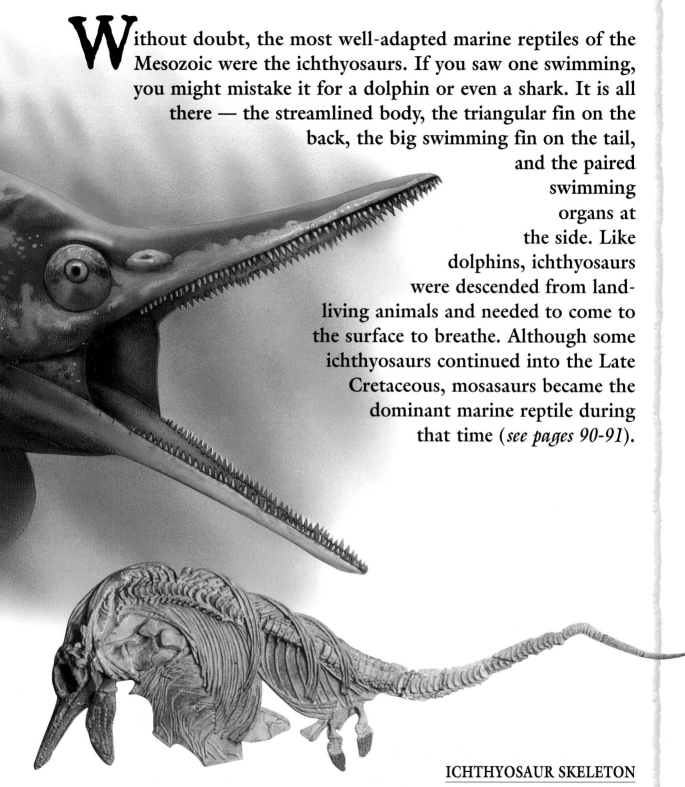

Without doubt, the most well-adapted marine reptiles of the Mesozoic were the ichthyosaurs. If you saw one swimming, you might mistake it for a dolphin or even a shark. It is all there — the streamlined body, the triangular fin on the back, the big swimming fin on the tail, and the paired swimming organs at the side. Like dolphins, ichthyosaurs were descended from land-living animals and needed to come to the surface to breathe. Although some ichthyosaurs continued into the Late Cretaceous, mosasaurs became the dominant marine reptile during that time (*see pages 90-91*).

ICHTHYOSAUR SKELETON

Entire skeletons of ichthyosaurs are relatively common, since these creatures were frequently fossilized. Many museums have complete ichthyosaur skeletons on display. This ichthyosaur is in the Bristol City Museum in England.

TRIASSIC 248-206 MYA	EARLY/MID JURASSIC 206-159 MYA	LATE JURASSIC 159-144 MYA	EARLY CRETACEOUS 144-97 MYA	LATE CRETACEOUS 97-65 MYA

A RANGE OF ICHTHYOSAURS

Before the standard dolphin shape of the ichthyosaur evolved, this creature came in many different shapes and sizes, particularly among the earlier ichthyosaurs in the Triassic seas. These different types had different lifestyles and swimming techniques. Some were long and narrow like eels, without a significant tail fin. They probably swam with a flying motion, like the plesiosaurs and penguins, and steered with their long tails. Some were the size of whales, with increased bone mass to make them heavier and able to swim in deep water for long periods. This range of Triassic forms soon settled to the classic dolphin shape of the Jurassic ichthyosaur.

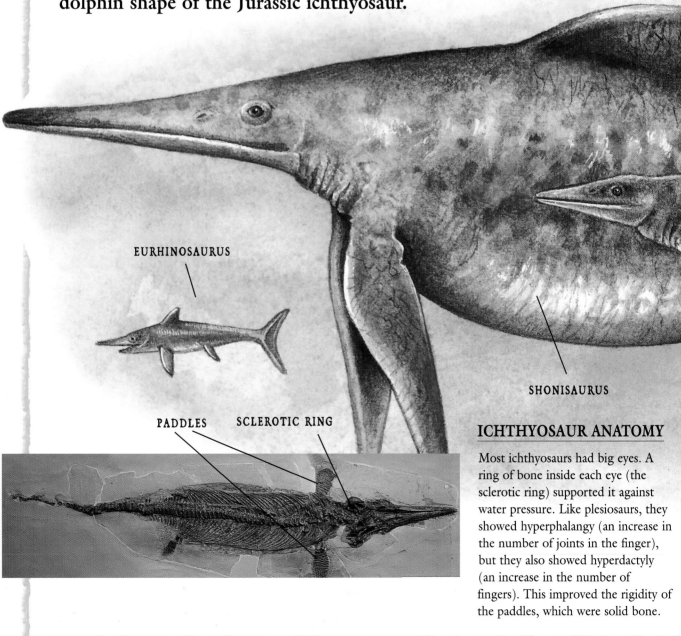

EURHINOSAURUS

SHONISAURUS

PADDLES   SCLEROTIC RING

ICHTHYOSAUR ANATOMY

Most ichthyosaurs had big eyes. A ring of bone inside each eye (the sclerotic ring) supported it against water pressure. Like plesiosaurs, they showed hyperphalangy (an increase in the number of joints in the finger), but they also showed hyperdactyly (an increase in the number of fingers). This improved the rigidity of the paddles, which were solid bone.

An ichthyosaur's swimming motion (at least that of the dolphin-shaped ichthyosaurs) depended on the complex interaction of thrust and the center of balance. The tail gave a forward and upward thrust directed through the center of balance, and the paddles adjusted the trim. Curving itself in a vertical plane, the ichthyosaur could dive and surface. The easiest way to turn would be to execute this movement and use its paddles to roll itself onto its side.

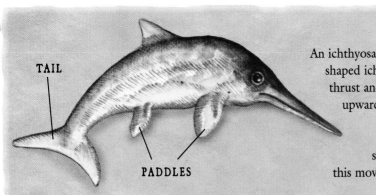

TAIL

PADDLES

TRIASSIC GIANT

A truly enormous Triassic ichthyosaur was discovered in British Columbia, Canada, in 1998. At 75 feet (23 m), it was longer than a sperm whale and approached the length of most blue whales. The skeleton is 30 percent longer than any other marine reptile so far discovered, and its head is 19 feet (5.8 m) long. It is being studied and does not yet have a name.

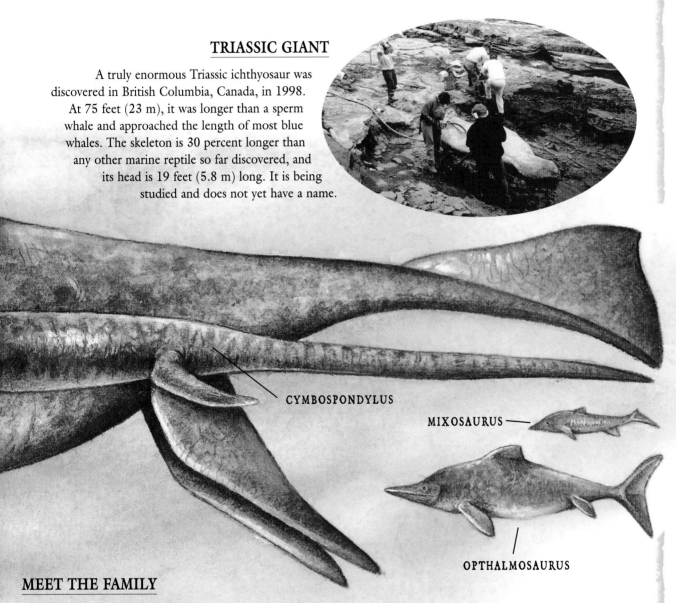

CYMBOSPONDYLUS

MIXOSAURUS

OPTHALMOSAURUS

MEET THE FAMILY

Probably the most primitive-looking ichthyosaur was *Cymbospondylus*, found in the Middle Triassic rocks of Nevada. Measuring 33 feet (10 m), it was a big animal, but its body was long and eel-like. *Mixosaurus*, found in Middle Triassic rocks from around the world, was still long and slim, but it showed the beginnings of the typical ichthyosaur tail. The 49-foot (15-m) monster *Shonisaurus*, from the late Triassic rocks of Nevada, was the biggest ichthyosaur known before the discovery of the Canadian giant *(see above)*. *Opthalmosaurus* was probably the most fishlike and had no teeth in its jaws. It may have fed on soft-bodied animals like squid. *Eurhinosaurus* had a swordfish-like beak on its upper jaw. It possibly used this beak for stunning fish prey.

TRIASSIC 248-206 MYA	EARLY/MID JURASSIC 206-159 MYA	LATE JURASSIC 159-144 MYA	EARLY CRETACEOUS 144-97 MYA	LATE CRETACEOUS 97-65 MYA

ICHTHYOSAURS - DISPELLING A MYTH

The fact that reptiles lay eggs on land is what distinguishes them from their ancestors, the amphibians. Occasionally, however, reptiles that live in harsh environments in which exposed eggs would be vulnerable tend to give birth to live young. Most of the modern reptiles that live in northern Europe, such as the common lizard, the slow worm, and the adder, bear live young. The ichthyosaurs also did this.

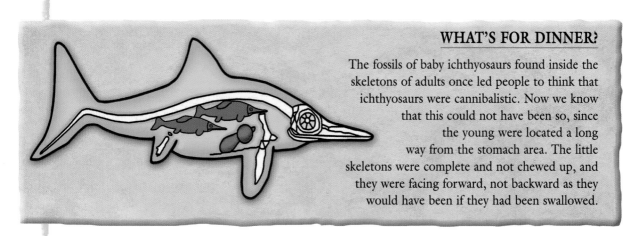

WHAT'S FOR DINNER?

The fossils of baby ichthyosaurs found inside the skeletons of adults once led people to think that ichthyosaurs were cannibalistic. Now we know that this could not have been so, since the young were located a long way from the stomach area. The little skeletons were complete and not chewed up, and they were facing forward, not backward as they would have been if they had been swallowed.

HOLZMADEN

In Late Jurassic times, a shallow sea with scattered islands covered most of northern Europe. To the north was low-lying land, and to the south, beyond a series of massive reefs formed by corals and sponges, lay the open ocean. The region of Holzmaden may have been a seasonal gathering place where ichthyosaurs came to give birth. We can tell much about the ichthyosaurs' anatomy and lifestyle from fossils found in the region. A large number of ichthyosaur remains shows baby ichthyosaurs emerging from the adult. These remains tell us that ichthyosaur birth was a very traumatic event that sometimes proved fatal for the mother.

TRIASSIC 248-206 MYA	EARLY/MID JURASSIC 206-159 MYA	LATE JURASSIC 159-144 MYA	EARLY CRETACEOUS 144-97 MYA	LATE CRETACEOUS 97-65 MYA

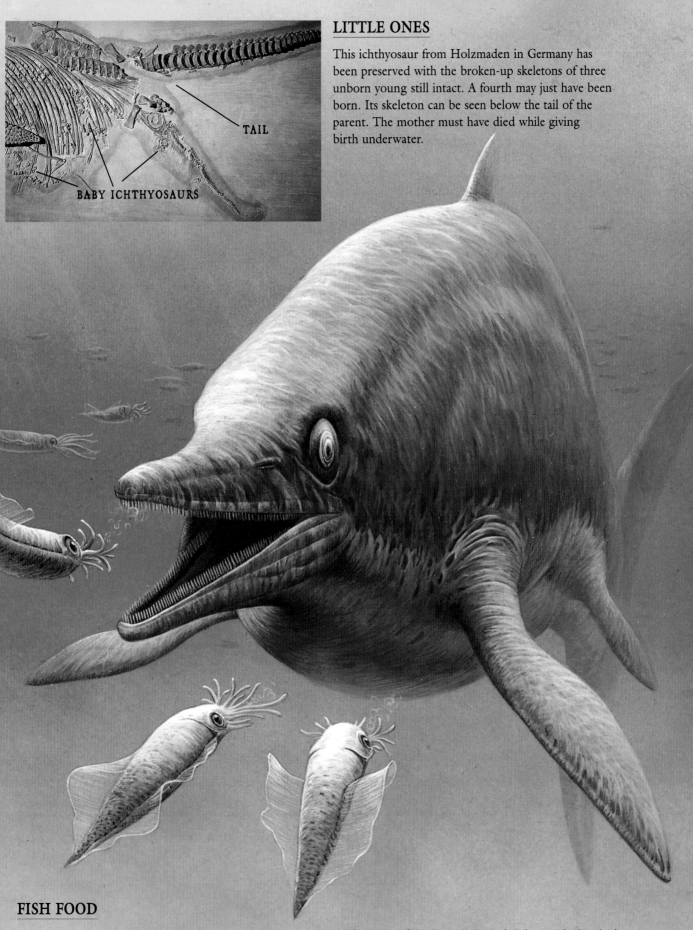

LITTLE ONES

This ichthyosaur from Holzmaden in Germany has been preserved with the broken-up skeletons of three unborn young still intact. A fourth may just have been born. Its skeleton can be seen below the tail of the parent. The mother must have died while giving birth underwater.

TAIL

BABY ICHTHYOSAURS

FISH FOOD

Belemnites were squidlike animals that swarmed in the warm shallow seas of the Jurassic Period. Like squid, they had tentacles that were armed with tiny hooks, but unlike squid, their bodies were stiffened with bullet-shaped internal shells. These shells are commonly found as fossils in Jurassic rocks. We know that many ichthyosaurs ate belemnites, because we have found masses of their indigestible hooks in the stomach areas of ichthyosaur fossils.

A SWIMMING LIZARD

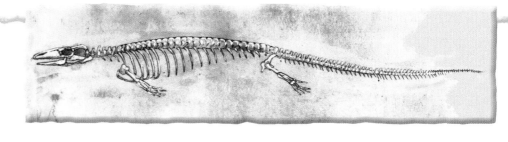

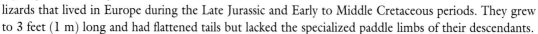

The aigalosaurs were ancestors of the mosasaurs. They were a group of swimming lizards that lived in Europe during the Late Jurassic and Early to Middle Cretaceous periods. They grew to 3 feet (1 m) long and had flattened tails but lacked the specialized paddle limbs of their descendants.

DINNER TIME

There is direct evidence that mosasaurs ate the abundant ammonites of the time. The ammonites were relatives of the modern squid and nautilus and displayed coiled shells that are very common as fossils. They lived throughout the Mesozoic in seas all over the world. One ammonite fossil has been found punctured by tooth marks that exactly match those of a small mosasaur. Evidently, the reptile had to bite the ammonite sixteen times before crushing the shell and reaching the animal.

FAMILY MEMBER?

The bones of *Mosasaurus* were very similar to those of the modern monitor lizard. Despite the extinction of individual species, the same lines of animals were continuing to develop into other forms. The concept of evolution that would explain such phenomena had not been developed when *Mosasaurus* was first studied.

GEORGES CUVIER

Baron Georges Cuvier (1769–1832) was impressed by the jawbones of an unknown giant reptile unearthed from underground quarries near the River Meuse. The French anatomist became convinced that there were once animals living on Earth that were completely unlike modern types and that these ancient animals were periodically wiped out by extinction events.

TRIASSIC 248-206 MYA	EARLY/MID JURASSIC 206-159 MYA	LATE JURASSIC 159-144 MYA	EARLY CRETACEOUS 144-97 MYA	LATE CRETACEOUS 97-65 MYA

MOSASAURS

In 1770, workmen in a chalk quarry near Maastricht in Holland uncovered a long-jawed, toothy skull. The owner of the land sued for possession — a circumstance that is all too common in the field of paleontology, even today. In 1794, the French army invaded Holland and, despite the owner's attempt to hide the skull in a cave, seized it and took it back to Paris. There it was studied by the legendary French anatomist Baron Georges Cuvier. By this time it had been identified as the skull of a huge reptile related to the modern monitor lizards. British geologist William Conybeare gave it the name *Mosasaurus* ("lizard from the Meuse").

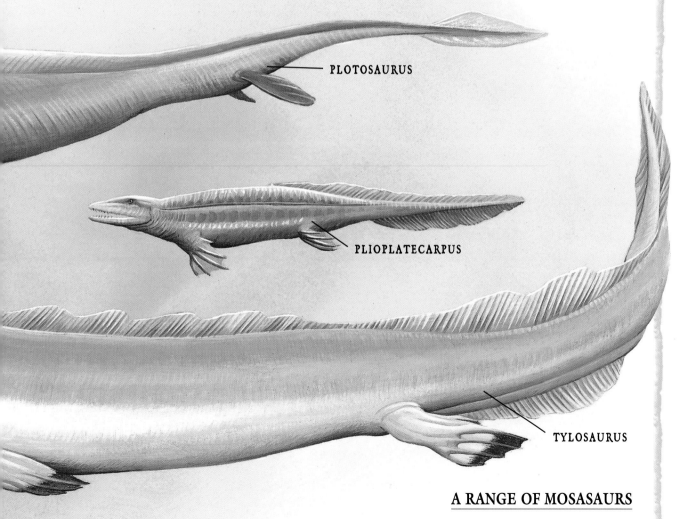

PLOTOSAURUS

PLIOPLATECARPUS

TYLOSAURUS

A RANGE OF MOSASAURS

Mosasaurs are known from Late Cretaceous deposits throughout the world. They were all based on a similar body plan and ranged in size from a few feet to monsters 33 feet (10 m) or more in length. Their heads were all very similar to those of the modern monitor lizard, and their teeth had adapted to snatch at fish or ammonites. An exception was *Globidens*, which had flattened, rounded teeth that were obviously adapted to a shellfish diet.

CROCODILES

Crocodiles have remained essentially unaltered since Late Triassic times. Throughout their history, however, crocodiles have adapted to many conditions. Some were long-legged and scampered about on land, while some ran on hind legs like little versions of their relatives, the dinosaurs. More significantly, some developed into sea-living forms showing the same adaptations as other sea-living reptiles — the sinuous bodies, the paddle legs, and the finned tails. These features were particularly important in Jurassic times.

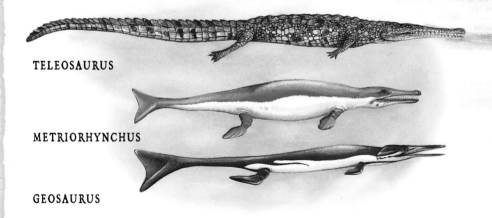

TELEOSAURUS

METRIORHYNCHUS

GEOSAURUS

A SELECTION OF SEA CROCS

Teleosaurus was a gharial-like sea crocodile. It was even longer and slimmer in build than *Steneosaurus. Metriorhynchus* was 10 feet(3 m) long and shows much more extreme adaptations to a seagoing way of life. It lacked the armored scales that we see on more conventional crocodiles. Its legs were converted into paddles that would have been almost useless on land. At the end of its tail the vertebral column was turned downward, showing that it had a swimming fin like an ichthyosaur. This was a true sea crocodile. *Geosaurus* had the same adaptations as *Metriorhynchus* but appeared somewhat later and, at 7 feet (2 m) long, was considerably smaller. It was much slimmer, and the jaws were even narrower.

CHAMPSOSAUR

PHYTOSAUR

CROCODILE

A GOOD SHAPE

Many semi-aquatic, meat-eating reptiles have crocodile shapes. The phytosaurs from the Late Triassic could be mistaken for crocodiles except for their nostrils, which were close to the eyes instead of at the tip of the snout. The champsosaurs from the Late Cretaceous of North America were also very crocodile-like, having the same lifestyle in the same habitat. None of these animals was closely related to another. This pattern is an example of "parallel evolution."

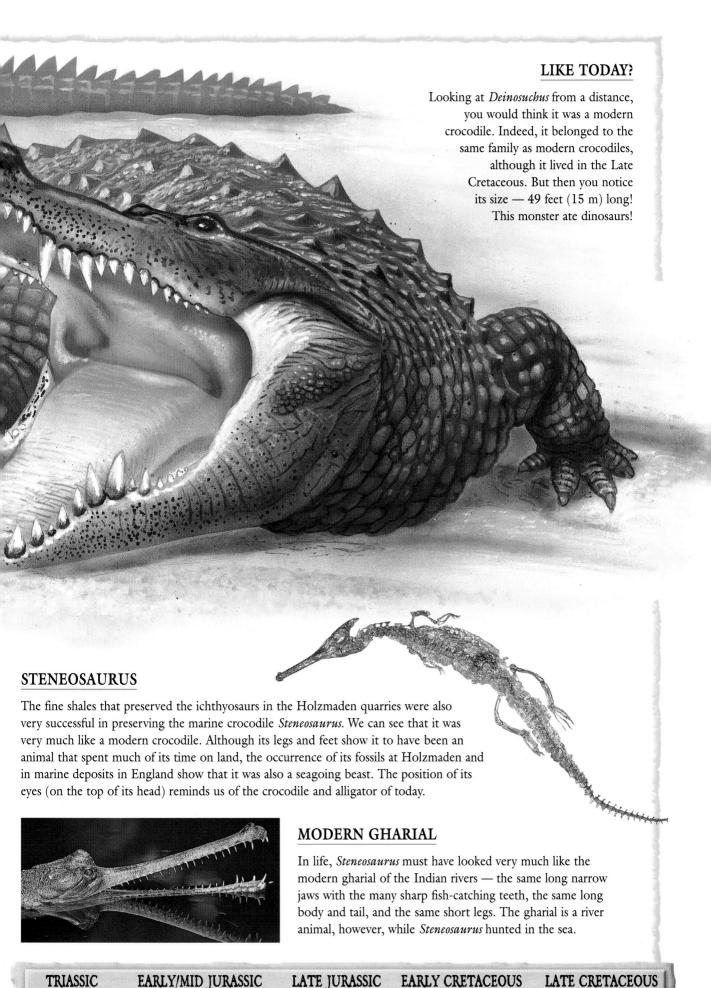

LIKE TODAY?

Looking at *Deinosuchus* from a distance, you would think it was a modern crocodile. Indeed, it belonged to the same family as modern crocodiles, although it lived in the Late Cretaceous. But then you notice its size — 49 feet (15 m) long! This monster ate dinosaurs!

STENEOSAURUS

The fine shales that preserved the ichthyosaurs in the Holzmaden quarries were also very successful in preserving the marine crocodile *Steneosaurus*. We can see that it was very much like a modern crocodile. Although its legs and feet show it to have been an animal that spent much of its time on land, the occurrence of its fossils at Holzmaden and in marine deposits in England show that it was also a seagoing beast. The position of its eyes (on the top of its head) reminds us of the crocodile and alligator of today.

MODERN GHARIAL

In life, *Steneosaurus* must have looked very much like the modern gharial of the Indian rivers — the same long narrow jaws with the many sharp fish-catching teeth, the same long body and tail, and the same short legs. The gharial is a river animal, however, while *Steneosaurus* hunted in the sea.

TRIASSIC 248-206 MYA	EARLY/MID JURASSIC 206-159 MYA	LATE JURASSIC 159-144 MYA	EARLY CRETACEOUS 144-97 MYA	LATE CRETACEOUS 97-65 MYA

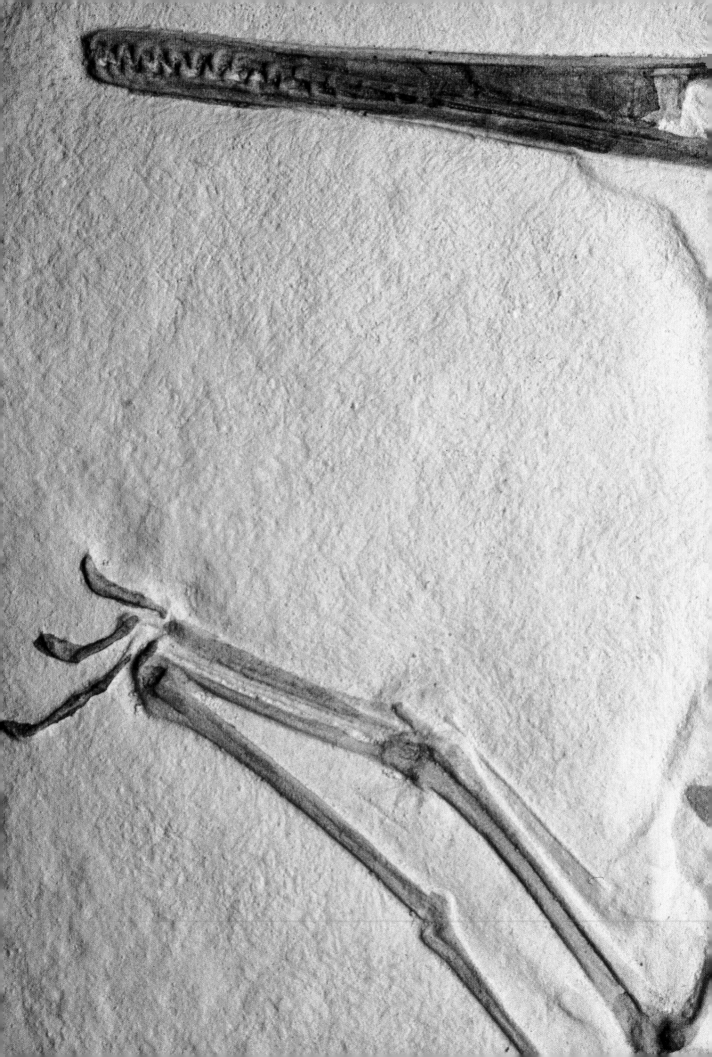

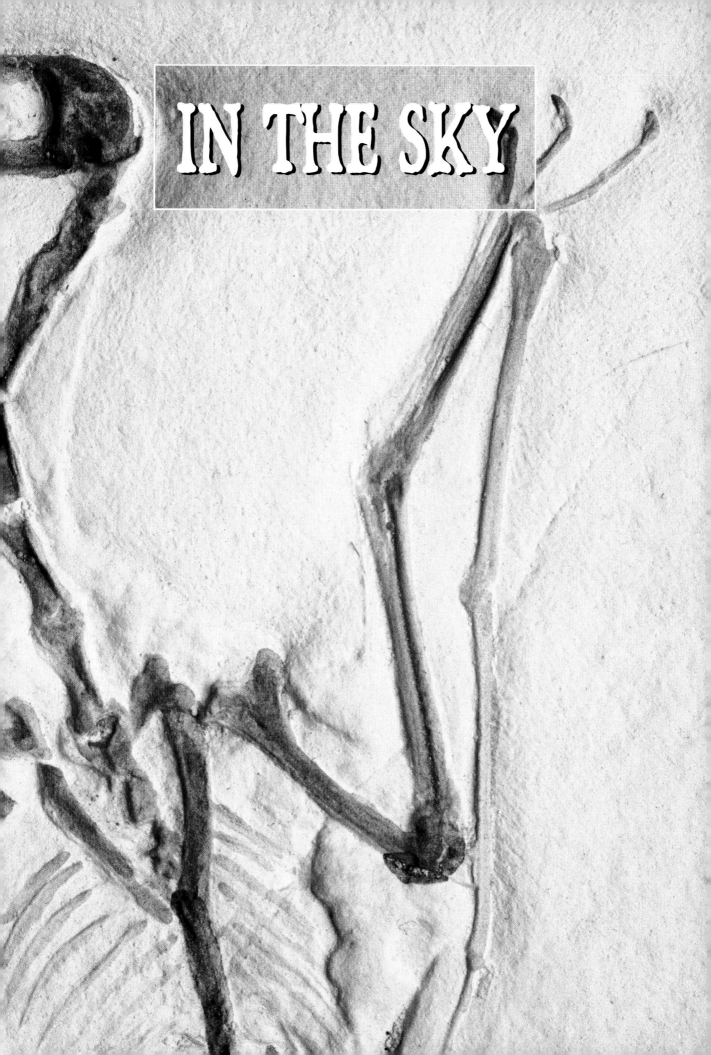

IN THE SKY

WING AND A PRAYER

The earliest flying reptile known was the Late Permian *Coelurosauravus*. It looked very much like a lizard, but its ribs were extended to the side and supported gliding wings made of skin. The modern flying lizard of Malaysia glides in exactly the same manner as *Coelurosauravus*.

KING OF THE SKIES

By Late Triassic times, gliders like *Coelurosauravus* had been replaced in importance by the pterosaurs. These famous flying reptiles were the first vertebrates to adapt to a life of active flight. They appeared at about the same time as the first dinosaurs and became extinct at the end of the Cretaceous Period. Pterosaur wings were made of reinforced skin stretched out on an arm and an elongated fourth finger.

EARLY BIRDS

Birds such as this *Sinornis* appeared about halfway through the time of the dinosaurs, evolving from the dinosaurs themselves. Birds continue to thrive and are the main flying vertebrates today. Their wings are made of a bony structure consisting of some of the fingers fused together and supporting feathers that fan from the arms.

THE PIONEERS

While the dinosaurs, fish, and mammals were colonizing the land and the sea in prehistoric times, the sky above was buzzing with activity. Early flyers were simple organisms, but nature gradually came up with more complex designs. First came the insects, which continue to flourish today. Next came the flying reptiles, gliding creatures that evolved from ground-living, lizardlike animals. These reptiles were replaced in importance by the pterosaurs, probably the most famous of the ancient flying reptiles. Finally, the first birds appeared halfway through the time of the dinosaurs and have continued to rule the skies to this day.

AMBER PERFECTION

The best fossils come from amber preservation. When an unwary insect gets stuck in the sticky resin that oozes from tree trunks, the resin engulfs the insect and preserves it perfectly. When the tree dies and becomes buried over a long period of time, the resin solidifies and becomes the mineral we call amber. The 1994 film *Jurassic Park* was based on the premise that foreign DNA could be taken from biting insects preserved in amber to recreate the creature that was bitten. While this might not be possible today, it is an exciting concept.

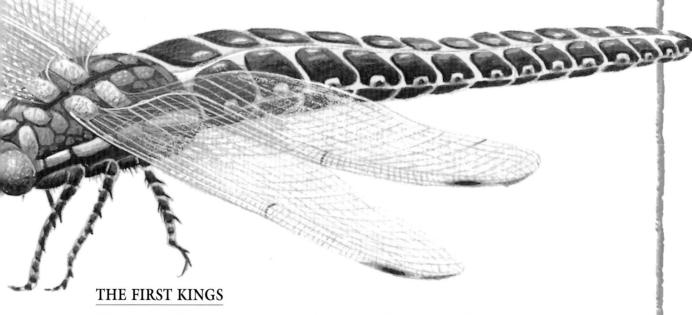

THE FIRST KINGS

Meganeura was like a dragonfly but much larger — the size of a parrot. Its wings were typical insect wings, consisting of a thin sheet of chitin supported by a network of rigid veins. *Meganeura* lived in the Carboniferous Period, not long after insects first evolved.

CARBONIFEROUS/PERMIAN 354-290/290-248 MYA	TRIASSIC 248-206 MYA	EARLY/MID JURASSIC 206-159 MYA	LATE JURASSIC 159-144 MYA	EARLY/LATE CRETACEOUS 144-65 MYA

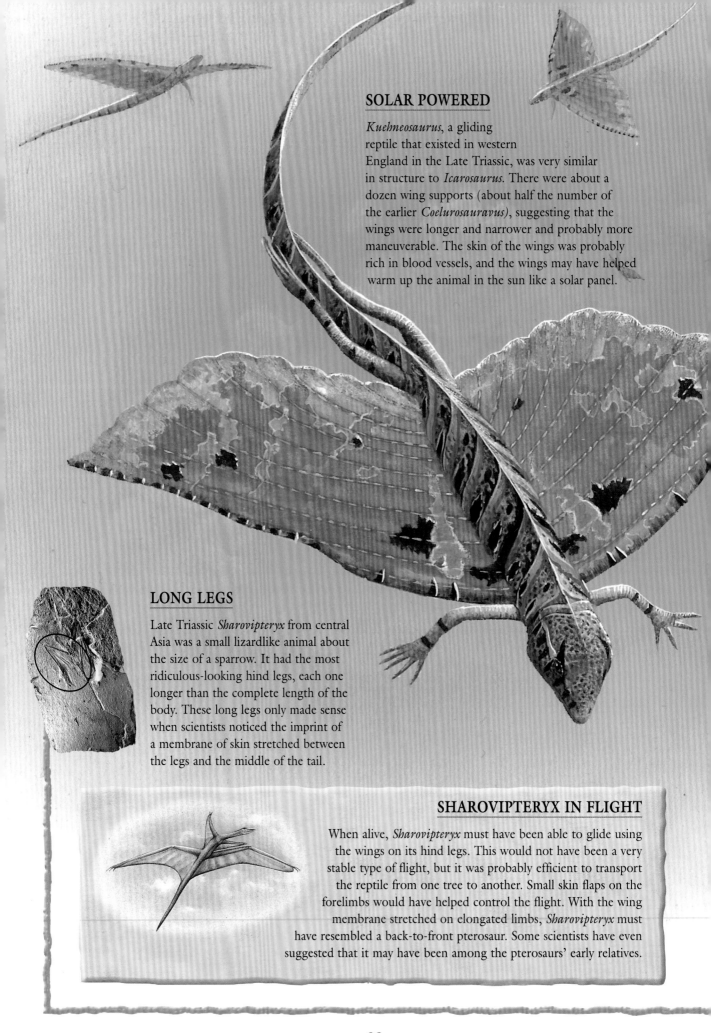

SOLAR POWERED

Kuehneosaurus, a gliding reptile that existed in western England in the Late Triassic, was very similar in structure to *Icarosaurus*. There were about a dozen wing supports (about half the number of the earlier *Coelurosauravus*), suggesting that the wings were longer and narrower and probably more maneuverable. The skin of the wings was probably rich in blood vessels, and the wings may have helped warm up the animal in the sun like a solar panel.

LONG LEGS

Late Triassic *Sharovipteryx* from central Asia was a small lizardlike animal about the size of a sparrow. It had the most ridiculous-looking hind legs, each one longer than the complete length of the body. These long legs only made sense when scientists noticed the imprint of a membrane of skin stretched between the legs and the middle of the tail.

SHAROVIPTERYX IN FLIGHT

When alive, *Sharovipteryx* must have been able to glide using the wings on its hind legs. This would not have been a very stable type of flight, but it was probably efficient to transport the reptile from one tree to another. Small skin flaps on the forelimbs would have helped control the flight. With the wing membrane stretched on elongated limbs, *Sharovipteryx* must have resembled a back-to-front pterosaur. Some scientists have even suggested that it may have been among the pterosaurs' early relatives.

EARLY FLYING REPTILES

The simplest kind of flight is a gliding flight — one that needs little muscular effort. All that is required is a lightness of body and some kind of structure that catches the air and allows the body to be carried along upon it, like a paper airplane. In modern times, we see this structure in flying squirrels, flying lizards, and even flying frogs. A number of flying reptiles populated the skies in Permian and Triassic times, and each one evolved independently from different reptile ancestors.

LONGISQUAMA

This fossil of the flying reptile *Longisquama* comes from Late Triassic central Asia. It had a completely different type of flying mechanism. A double row of long scales stuck up along the backbone, each scale forming a shallow V-shape along its midline. When spread, the scales would have overlapped like the feathers of birds (which appeared 60 million years later) to give a continuous gliding surface.

SCALES

A FAMOUS FIND

Three schoolboys in New Jersey discovered a famous specimen of Late Triassic *Icarosaurus*. The partial skeleton shows it to have been a lizardlike animal with long projections from its ribs. The angles at which the rib extensions lay suggested that the wings could have been folded back out of the way when the animal was at rest. Several decades after the discovery, one of the finders realized that under U.S. law the specimen belonged to those who made the discovery, and the specimen is now lost to science, having disappeared into a private collection.

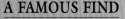

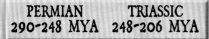

PERMIAN	TRIASSIC	EARLY/MID JURASSIC	LATE JURASSIC	EARLY/LATE CRETACEOUS
290-248 MYA	248-206 MYA	206-159 MYA	159-144 MYA	144-65 MYA

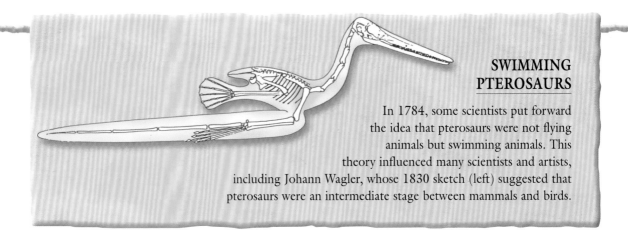

SWIMMING PTEROSAURS

In 1784, some scientists put forward the idea that pterosaurs were not flying animals but swimming animals. This theory influenced many scientists and artists, including Johann Wagler, whose 1830 sketch (left) suggested that pterosaurs were an intermediate stage between mammals and birds.

DEVILISH PTEROSAURS

In 1840, British geologist Thomas Hawkins published a book on the fossil sea reptiles (the ichthyosaurs and plesiosaurs) that had been discovered up to that time. The frontispiece of the book was an engraving by John Martin, an English painter of biblical and historical subjects. It was a nightmare scene in which he depicted monstrous ichthyosaurs, plesiosaurs, and pterosaurs that resembled bat-winged demons.

FURRY PTEROSAURS

A surprisingly modern interpretation of pterosaurs was drawn in 1843 by Edward Newman. He regarded pterosaurs as flying marsupials. Although the mouse ears are inaccurate, the furry bodies and the predatory lifestyle are in keeping with how we now regard these creatures.

VICTORIAN TERRORS

The concrete pterosaurs (or "pterodactyles" as they were then called) erected on the grounds of the Crystal Palace in south London in 1854 tell us that most Victorians still viewed these creatures as winged dragons. These statues were more delicate than the surrounding statues of dinosaurs and sea animals, and unfortunately most were badly damaged or destroyed by the 1930s.

THE DISCOVERY OF THE PTEROSAURS

The first pterosaur fossil to have been scientifically studied was an almost perfect skeleton from the lithographic limestone quarries of Solnhofen, Germany, discovered between 1767 and 1784. Although the skeleton was nearly complete, it was impossible to compare it with any animal alive at the time, so the find remained a mystery. Seventeen years later, the French pioneer naturalist Baron Georges Cuvier guessed that it was a flying reptile. Since that date, scientists have come up with many different ideas of what pterosaurs were and how they lived.

JURASSIC BATS?

English geologist Sir Henry De la Beche produced a drawing in 1830 showing animal life in the Jurassic (then called Liassic) sea of southern England. Life in the sea consisted of swimming reptiles, fish, and ammonites. In the air were flying pterosaurs, which De la Beche depicted as batlike creatures, with their wing membranes stretching all the way to their feet.

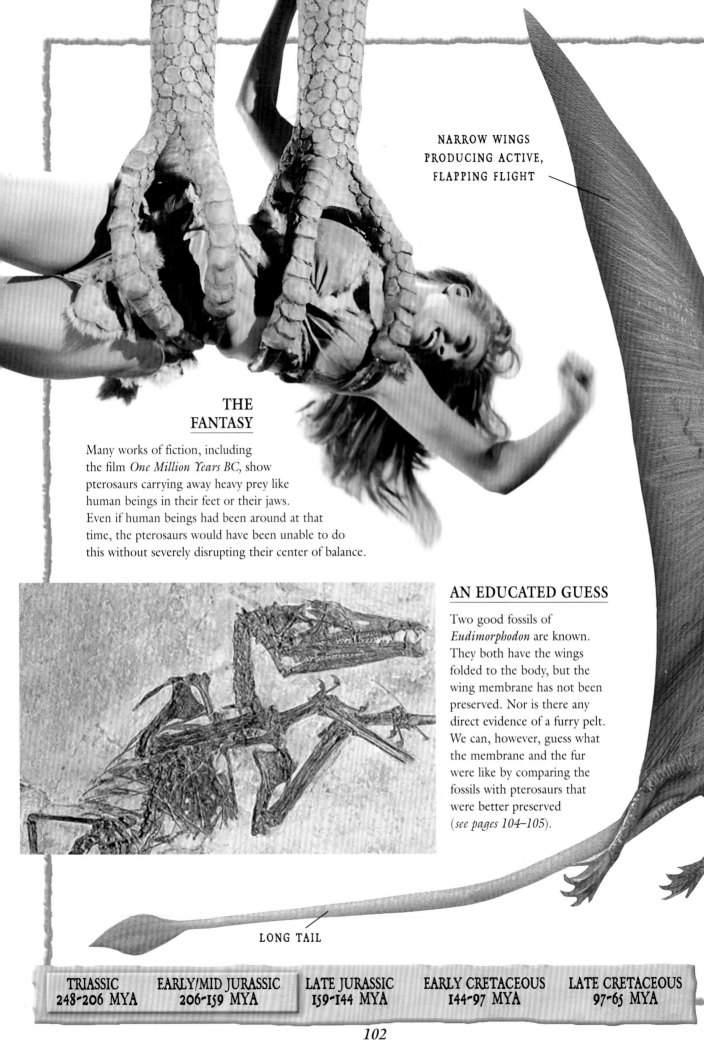

NARROW WINGS
PRODUCING ACTIVE,
FLAPPING FLIGHT

THE FANTASY

Many works of fiction, including the film *One Million Years BC*, show pterosaurs carrying away heavy prey like human beings in their feet or their jaws. Even if human beings had been around at that time, the pterosaurs would have been unable to do this without severely disrupting their center of balance.

AN EDUCATED GUESS

Two good fossils of *Eudimorphodon* are known. They both have the wings folded to the body, but the wing membrane has not been preserved. Nor is there any direct evidence of a furry pelt. We can, however, guess what the membrane and the fur were like by comparing the fossils with pterosaurs that were better preserved (*see pages 104–105*).

LONG TAIL

TRIASSIC 248-206 MYA	EARLY/MID JURASSIC 206-159 MYA	LATE JURASSIC 159-144 MYA	EARLY CRETACEOUS 144-97 MYA	LATE CRETACEOUS 97-65 MYA

EUDIMORPHODON

Eudimorphodon had all the physical attributes of the rhamphorhynchoids. It had long, narrow wings made of skin supported by rods of gristle and a wing span of about 3 feet (1 meter). Because of its variety of teeth, it could easily catch and eat fish, and its furry body kept this creature warm and helped make possible its constantly active lifestyle.

THE EARLIEST PTEROSAUR

The pterosaurs were the most important of the flying animals in Triassic, Jurassic, and Cretaceous times. Once they evolved, they quickly adopted all the features that were to remain with the group for the rest of their existence. Pterosaurs fall into two groups. The more primitive group — the rhamphorhynchoids — had long tails, short wrist bones, and narrow wings. Appearing in Triassic times, they were the first to evolve. The other group — the pterodactyloids — evolved later, toward the end of the Jurassic.

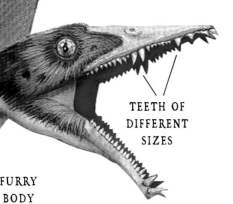

SHORT WRIST BONES

TEETH OF DIFFERENT SIZES

FURRY BODY

WING MUSCLES

Pterosaurs must have had a flying action like that of modern bats or birds (right). The arrangement of their shoulder bones and wing bones show that the muscles facilitated active, flapping flight.

CATCHING PREY

Many pterosaurs caught fish, and, judging by its teeth, *Eudimorphodon* was one of them. The balance of the animal in flight was so delicate that it would not have been able to fly with a fish in its mouth. The pterosaur had to have swallowed the fish immediately to get it to its center of balance.

DIMORPHODON SKELETON

The skeletons of *Dimorphodon* fall to pieces and are crushed easily, because they are made up of the finest struts of bone. Nevertheless, two good *Dimorphodon* specimens have been found, both of them now in the Natural History Museum in London.

JURASSIC SKIES

Above the Early Jurassic shorelines the air was thick with wheeling pterosaurs. They were all of the long-tailed rhamphorhynchoid type. Within a few million years these creatures would be replaced by a new pterosaur group — the short-tailed, long-necked, long-wristed pterodactyloids.

BIG HEADS

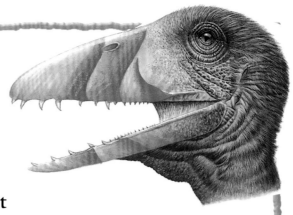

Rhamphorhynchoid pterosaurs ruled the skies during the early Jurassic Period. The earliest Jurassic pterosaur known was discovered in 1828 by the famous professional collector Mary Anning. It was given the name *Dimorphodon* because of its two types of teeth. Scientists today are still in disagreement over many of its features. These disagreements are typical of our lack of knowledge of the pterosaurs in general.

BRILLIANT BEAK

Dimorphodon had two different types of teeth that were good for grabbing and holding slippery prey such as fish. The skull was very high and narrow and consisted of windows separated by fine struts of bone. The sides of the head were very likely brightly colored for signaling, just like the beaks of modern tall-beaked birds, such as puffins or toucans.

ON THE GROUND

We know that pterosaurs like *Dimorphodon* were very adept at flight, but we are not sure how they moved around when they were not flying. The old theory was that pterosaurs crawled like lizards, while some scientists saw them as running on their hind legs like birds, with their wings folded out of the way. However, footprints in lake sediments from South America attributed to pterosaurs show the marks of the hind feet walking in a narrow track, with marks seemingly made by the claws of the forelimbs in a wider track on each side. This suggests that pterosaurs were walking upright, using the arms like crutches or walking sticks. A final theory suggests that because of their similarity to bats, perhaps they did not come to the ground at all but hung upside down from trees.

TRIASSIC 248-206 MYA	EARLY/MID JURASSIC 206-159 MYA	LATE JURASSIC 159-144 MYA	EARLY CRETACEOUS 144-97 MYA	LATE CRETACEOUS 97-65 MYA

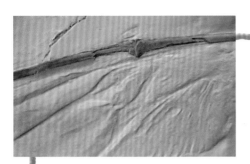

SOFT COVERINGS

WING STRUCTURE

The wing membrane of a pterosaur was stiffened by fine rods of gristle that fanned out from the arm and hand to the wing's trailing edge. The pattern of the gristle stiffening is the same as the arrangement of a bird's flight feathers and the supporting fingers of a bat's wing.

Most fossils are of sea-living animals, because sea-living animals have a better chance of falling to the seabed and eventually becoming entombed in sedimentary rock. However, many pterosaurs lived in coastal areas or around lakes and fell into the water when they died. Sometimes they were fossilized in environments that preserved the finest of details, such as wing membranes and fur.

A MODERN INTERPRETATION?

Many think that birds are the modern equivalent of the pterosaurs. The pterosaur has more in common with the modern bat than with any bird, however, particularly with its fur and membranous wings. Pterosaurs and birds shared the Cretaceous skies, but bats did not evolve until pterosaurs died out.

THE BEST PRESERVED

This *Rhamphorhynchus* from the Solnhofen deposits in Germany is one of the best preserved pterosaur fossils we have. Even the structure of its wing membrane is visible.

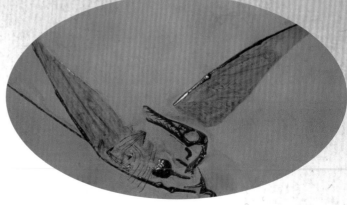

TRIASSIC 248-206 MYA	EARLY/MID JURASSIC 206-159 MYA	LATE JURASSIC 159-144 MYA	EARLY CRETACEOUS 144-97 MYA	LATE CRETACEOUS 97-65 MYA

HOW WERE THE WINGS ATTACHED?

A great deal of uncertainty surrounds the question of just how the pterosaur's wings were attached to the animal. Some scientists think that the wings stretched from the arms and fourth finger to the body and did not touch the hind limbs. Other scientists think that the wings were attached to the hind limbs at the knee. Others feel that the wings may have stretched right down to the ankles.

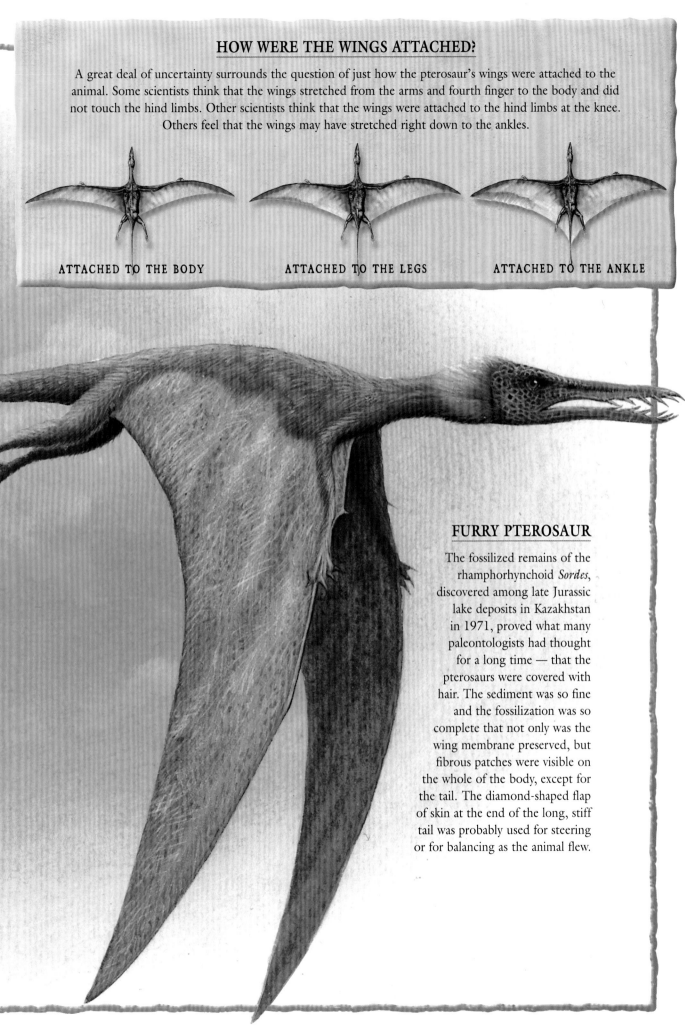

ATTACHED TO THE BODY   ATTACHED TO THE LEGS   ATTACHED TO THE ANKLE

FURRY PTEROSAUR

The fossilized remains of the rhamphorhynchoid *Sordes*, discovered among late Jurassic lake deposits in Kazakhstan in 1971, proved what many paleontologists had thought for a long time — that the pterosaurs were covered with hair. The sediment was so fine and the fossilization was so complete that not only was the wing membrane preserved, but fibrous patches were visible on the whole of the body, except for the tail. The diamond-shaped flap of skin at the end of the long, stiff tail was probably used for steering or for balancing as the animal flew.

When the British scientist Charles Darwin visited the Galapagos islands in the 19th century, he was struck by the variety of different beak shapes among one species of finch. Different shapes supported different lifestyles — heavy beaks for cracking seeds and short beaks for pecking insects, and so on. This revelation trigged Darwin's theory of evolution — the idea that, over millions of years, creatures could evolve to adapt to their surroundings. The variation in shape of the various *Pterodactylus* species fits in perfectly with Darwin's theory.

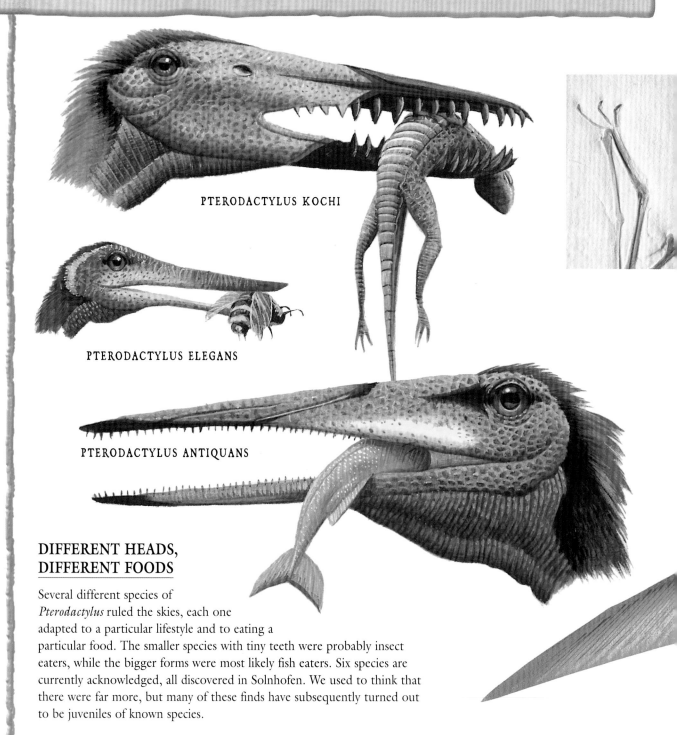

PTERODACTYLUS KOCHI

PTERODACTYLUS ELEGANS

PTERODACTYLUS ANTIQUANS

DIFFERENT HEADS, DIFFERENT FOODS

Several different species of *Pterodactylus* ruled the skies, each one adapted to a particular lifestyle and to eating a particular food. The smaller species with tiny teeth were probably insect eaters, while the bigger forms were most likely fish eaters. Six species are currently acknowledged, all discovered in Solnhofen. We used to think that there were far more, but many of these finds have subsequently turned out to be juveniles of known species.

TRIASSIC 248-206 MYA	EARLY/MID JURASSIC 206-159 MYA	LATE JURASSIC 159-144 MYA	EARLY CRETACEOUS 144-97 MYA	LATE CRETACEOUS 97-65 MYA

THE MOST FAMOUS

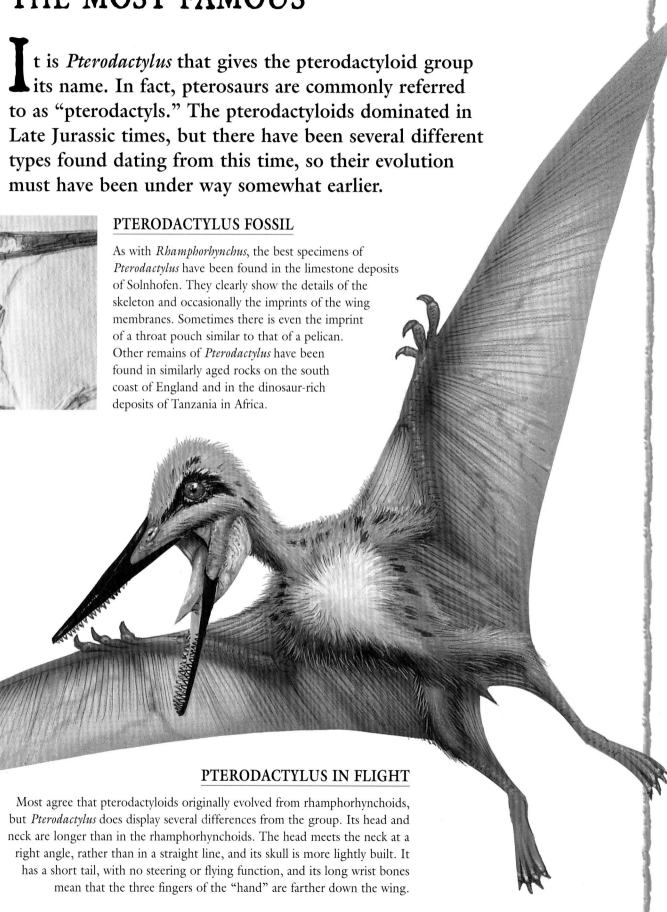

It is *Pterodactylus* that gives the pterodactyloid group its name. In fact, pterosaurs are commonly referred to as "pterodactyls." The pterodactyloids dominated in Late Jurassic times, but there have been several different types found dating from this time, so their evolution must have been under way somewhat earlier.

PTERODACTYLUS FOSSIL

As with *Rhamphorhynchus*, the best specimens of *Pterodactylus* have been found in the limestone deposits of Solnhofen. They clearly show the details of the skeleton and occasionally the imprints of the wing membranes. Sometimes there is even the imprint of a throat pouch similar to that of a pelican. Other remains of *Pterodactylus* have been found in similarly aged rocks on the south coast of England and in the dinosaur-rich deposits of Tanzania in Africa.

PTERODACTYLUS IN FLIGHT

Most agree that pterodactyloids originally evolved from rhamphorhynchoids, but *Pterodactylus* does display several differences from the group. Its head and neck are longer than in the rhamphorhynchoids. The head meets the neck at a right angle, rather than in a straight line, and its skull is more lightly built. It has a short tail, with no steering or flying function, and its long wrist bones mean that the three fingers of the "hand" are farther down the wing.

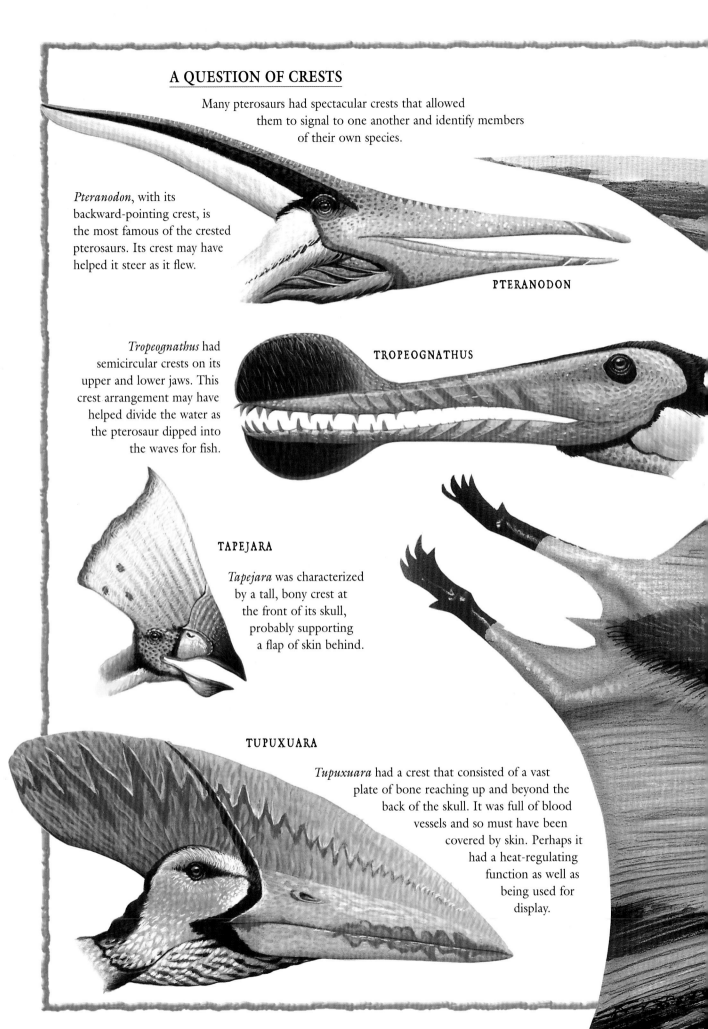

A QUESTION OF CRESTS

Many pterosaurs had spectacular crests that allowed them to signal to one another and identify members of their own species.

Pteranodon, with its backward-pointing crest, is the most famous of the crested pterosaurs. Its crest may have helped it steer as it flew.

PTERANODON

Tropeognathus had semicircular crests on its upper and lower jaws. This crest arrangement may have helped divide the water as the pterosaur dipped into the waves for fish.

TROPEOGNATHUS

TAPEJARA

Tapejara was characterized by a tall, bony crest at the front of its skull, probably supporting a flap of skin behind.

TUPUXUARA

Tupuxuara had a crest that consisted of a vast plate of bone reaching up and beyond the back of the skull. It was full of blood vessels and so must have been covered by skin. Perhaps it had a heat-regulating function as well as being used for display.

HEADS & CRESTS

Birds are in great abundance today. They range from perching birds and swimming birds to wading birds and hunting birds. Modern birds have a variety of different heads and beaks — deep, strong beaks for cracking nuts; long, pointed beaks for probing mud; short, sharp beaks for pecking insects; and hooked beaks for tearing flesh. This variety was just as pronounced among the pterodactyloids. During their time on Earth, they diversified into different types, with different head shapes to suit different lifestyles.

DSUNGARIPTERUS RESTORED

We can usually tell how an animal lived and what it ate by looking at its jaws. *Dsungaripterus*, which we think lived in Late Jurassic and Early Cretaceous Africa, probably ate shellfish. The narrow, pointed jaws could have been used for digging out shellfish from rocky crannies, and the shells would have been crushed by the toothlike knobs in the back of their jaws. The crest could have been brightly colored and was probably used for signaling other pterosaurs.

TRIASSIC	EARLY/MID JURASSIC	LATE JURASSIC	EARLY CRETACEOUS	LATE CRETACEOUS
248-206 MYA	206-159 MYA	159-144 MYA	144-97 MYA	97-65 MYA

PTERANODON SKELETON

This partial skeleton of the giant pterosaur *Pteranodon* was found in Cretaceous rocks in Kansas. It shows a skull fragment, the bones of the wing finger, and the complete hind legs. The whole skeleton was extremely light in weight, and the bones had openings to allow oxygen into air sacks connected to the lungs. We see this system in modern birds.

QUETZALCOATLUS

PTERANODON

ARGENTAVIS

A FLIGHT OF MONSTERS

Pteranodon has long been thought of as the largest of the pterosaurs. The biggest species of *Pteranodon* had a wingspan of about 30 feet (9 m). In the 1970s, however, remains from an even larger pterosaur were found in Upper Cretaceous rocks in Texas. It was given the name *Quetzalcoatlus*, after the flying serpent from Aztec mythology. All sorts of estimates were made about the size of this beast. The current estimate is that it had a wingspan of about 36–39 feet (11–12 m). The biggest bird known is the condorlike *Argentavis* from Argentina, which existed around 35 million years ago. It had a wingspan of 25 feet (7.5 m). Among living birds, the royal albatross has the biggest wingspan, reaching 10 feet (3 m).

THE BIGGEST

Pteranodon was discovered in the 1870s in the Upper Cretaceous beds of Kansas. It had a wingspan of more than 30 feet (9 m). This discovery occurred before the age of powered aviation, and science was astounded by the idea that anything this large could fly. Today its size seems fairly modest when we compare it with more recent discoveries.

THE BIGGEST — FOR THE MOMENT

The current record holder is *Arambourgiania*, a pterodactyloid that may have had a wingspan of about 39 feet (12 m). It had an extremely long neck, and when the neck bones were first found they were thought to have been the long finger bones that supported the wing. The original name given to this creature was *Titanopteryx*, but scientists had already given that name to something else, so its title had to be changed.

THE SMALLEST — FOR THE MOMENT

At the other end of the scale, tiny *Anurognathus* holds the record for the smallest known pterosaur. It had a wingspan of about 2 feet (50 centimeters). Its short head contained little peg-like teeth that were ideal for catching and crushing insects. Despite its short pterodactyloid-like tail, it is actually a member of the more primitive rhamphorhynchoids. Only one skeleton has been found, in the Late Jurassic Solnhofen deposits.

TRIASSIC	EARLY/MID JURASSIC	LATE JURASSIC	EARLY CRETACEOUS	LATE CRETACEOUS
248-206 MYA	206-159 MYA	159-144 MYA	144-97 MYA	97-65 MYA

7

THE FIRST BIRD

In 1859, Charles Darwin published *The Origin of Species* and created a sensation. How could animals have evolved into different types over a long period if they had all been created at one time, as it says in the Bible? The scientific community found itself in opposition to the overpowering influence of traditional biblical teaching. Then, two years later, a remarkable fossil was discovered in the quarries of Solnhofen. It was obviously a dinosaur, but it featured bird's wings and was covered with feathers. Here were the remains of a creature that appeared to represent a stage in the evolution of birds from dinosaurs. Today, few scientists dispute the notion that *Archaeopteryx* (as this creature was named) evolved from dinosaur ancestors.

FEATHER

The first *Archaeopteryx* fossil to be found was no more than a feather. By itself, it looks like nothing unusual. It is a perfectly conventional flight feather as found on a modern bird. The main support is a vane that is off-center, showing that it is from a wing and used for flight. The filaments forming the vane of the feather had rows of hooks that enabled them to connect with one another and give stability — just as in a modern bird. A downy portion at the base provided insulation — also as in birds. About a year later, the first partial *Archaeopteryx* skeleton was found.

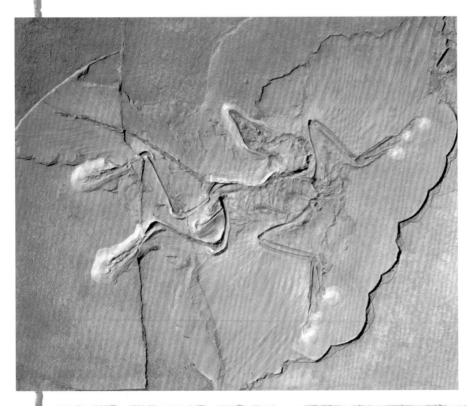

VINDICATING DARWIN

Eight *Archaeopteryx* fossils have been found so far, all from the Solnhofen quarries, ranging in quality from a single feather to an almost complete bony skeleton with feathers. One was found in a private collection, having been misidentified as the small dinosaur *Compsognathus*. This specimen did not show the feathers, and the misidentification points out the resemblance between primitive birds and their dinosaur ancestors.

THE LIVING ARCHAEOPTERYX

Had we seen *Archaeopteryx* in life, fluttering away from us, there would be no doubt in our minds that we were looking at a bird, though a rather clumsy one. However, a closer look would reveal a set of toothed jaws, as in a dinosaur, instead of the usual bird beak. The tail appeared to be paddle-shaped, unlike a modern bird's muscular stump with a bunch of feathers. This tail was a stiff, straight rod, like a dinosaur's tail, with feathers growing from each side. The final oddity would be the claws, three of them protruding from the leading edge of the wing. All in all, *Archaeopteryx* would have appeared part bird, part dinosaur.

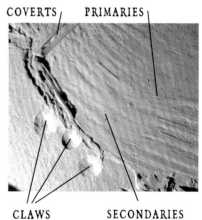

COVERTS PRIMARIES

CLAWS SECONDARIES

THE WING

The wing of *Archaeopteryx* was no halfway measure. Apart from the clawed fingers, it was identical in structure to the wing of a modern flying bird, with the elongated fingerlike primary feathers, bunched secondaries, and coverts streamlining the whole structure. The wing muscles would have been weaker than those of a modern bird, since there was no strong breastbone to anchor them. But the flying action must have been the same.

TRIASSIC	EARLY/MID JURASSIC	LATE JURASSIC	EARLY CRETACEOUS	LATE CRETACEOUS
248-206 MYA	206-159 MYA	159-144 MYA	144-97 MYA	97-65 MYA

CAUDIPTERYX'S ENVIRONMENT

Caudipteryx (foreground), part of the Chinese "Gang of Three," lived in an environment like the one shown above. Forests of conifers and ginkgoes, with an undergrowth of ferns and cycads, provided refuge and food for many different animals in Late Jurassic and Early Cretaceous China. Lizards and small mammals scampered through the undergrowth, and little feathered theropod dinosaurs hunted between the trees. The air was colonized by birds (some resembling modern types), while on the ground raced several different half-dinosaur, half-bird creatures.

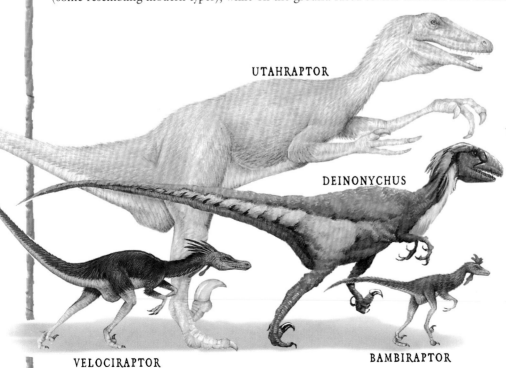

UTAHRAPTOR

DEINONYCHUS

VELOCIRAPTOR

BAMBIRAPTOR

MANIRAPTORAN DINOSAURS

The group of meat-eating dinosaurs known as the maniraptorans has always been viewed as birdlike. Attempts have been made to put them on the ancestral tree of the birds, but the problem is that, being Late Cretaceous dinosaurs, they lived much later than *Archaeopteryx*, which most scientists consider the first bird. Perhaps the maniraptorans evolved from *Archaeopteryx* or *Archaeopteryx*-like birds that lost their ability to fly. If that were true, they would have been very much like the Chinese "Gang of Three."

CHINESE "GANG OF THREE"

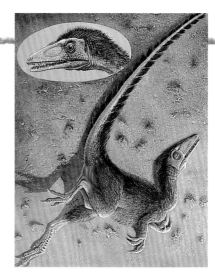

Across the contemporary European-Asian landmass, where China's Liaoning Province now lies, a series of forest-shrouded inland lakes produced fossils that were just as spectacular as those from Solnhofen. These include three kinds of animal that, like *Archaeopteryx*, show the evolutionary connection between birds and dinosaurs. Only recently, with improved scientific exchanges between China and the West, has their significance been fully appreciated.

SINOSAUROPTERYX

One of the little dinosaurs present in Liaoning Province was *Sinosauropteryx*. It seems to have been covered with fur or feathers. The fossil preservation is so good that a kind of downy fuzz is visible around the bones. Although there is still some dissent, most scientists are convinced that this represents a covering of "protofeathers," structures partway between hair, like that of a mammal, and feathers, like those of a bird.

SINOSAUROPTERYX FOSSIL

Only the downy covering on this skeleton shows *Sinosauropteryx* to have been related to the birds. Apart from that, it is pure meat-eating dinosaur. The long legs and tail show it to have been a swift-running animal, while the short arms displayed three claws. Three skeletons of *Sinosauropteryx* have been found, and their stomach contents show that they hunted lizards and small mammals.

HALF-BIRD, HALF-DINOSAUR

Another small animal was *Protarchaeoteryx*. It was about the same size as *Sinosauropteryx*, but it had a short tail and much longer arms. It was also covered with fuzz, and although the only skeleton found was very jumbled, there seemed to be long feathers along the arms and tail. The feathers on the arms would have given a winglike structure, but it would not have been sufficient to give the animal any power of flight.

TRIASSIC 248-206 MYA	EARLY/MID JURASSIC 206-159 MYA	LATE JURASSIC 159-144 MYA	EARLY CRETACEOUS 144-97 MYA	LATE CRETACEOUS 97-65 MYA

THE FIRST BEAK

Confuciusornis is the first beaked bird that we know of. A beak is a much more practical, lightweight alternative to the heavy teeth and jaws of a reptile. It consists of a sliver of bone, sheathed in a lightweight, horny substance that combines strength with lightness. Anything that reduces weight is an advantage to a flying animal.

— ALULA

FLIGHT CONTROL

Eoalulavis, from Early Cretaceous lake deposits in Spain, is the first bird that we know to have carried an alula. An alula is a tuft of feathers on the leading edge of the wing, more or less where our thumb is. With very small movements of this structure, the passage of air over the wing can be altered considerably, and this makes flight much more controllable. Although all modern birds have this feature, fossils of *Eoalulavis* are unclear about whether the bird had other advanced features, such as a beak or a pygostyle.

CONFUCIUSORNIS FOSSIL

Many hundreds of fossils of *Confuciusornis* have been uncovered at the Liaoning site in China. Some are so well preserved that the details of the plumage are clear. Some have long tail feathers, like those of a bird of paradise, while others have none. This suggests that, like modern birds, the males had much more flamboyant plumage than the females.

TRIASSIC 248-206 MYA	EARLY/MID JURASSIC 206-159 MYA	LATE JURASSIC 159-144 MYA	EARLY CRETACEOUS 144-97 MYA	LATE CRETACEOUS 97-65 MYA

TOWARD MODERN BIRDS

For all its fine feathers, *Archaeopteryx* was still mostly dinosaur. It had a long reptilian tail, fingers on the wings, and a jaw full of teeth. Modern birds have stumpy tails called pygostyles supporting long feathers. Their wing fingers have completely disappeared, and they also have beaks instead of jaws and teeth. These are all weight-saving adaptations, evolved to make the bird as light as possible so that it can fly more efficiently. These features seem to have appeared at different times during the time of the dinosaurs.

A MODERN TAIL

Iberomesornis, a fossil bird from Upper Cretaceous rocks in Spain, is the earliest bird known to have a pygostyle tail. This structure consists of a muscular stump from which the tail feathers grow in a fan arrangement. The muscles of the pygostyle can spread the tail feathers out or bunch them together, helping control flight or make a display for courting purposes.

THE PERCHING FOOT

Birds that live in trees usually have feet in which the first toe is turned backward, enabling the foot to grasp a small branch so the bird can perch. An early example of a perching foot is found in *Changchengornis*, a close relative of *Confuciusornis* that is also found in the Liaoning rocks. This bird also had a hooked beak, suggesting that it was a meat eater, like a modern hawk.

Hesperornis was a swimming bird of Late Cretaceous North America. As big as a human, it must have looked something like a penguin, but with no forelimbs at all and a long beak full of teeth. This leg bone was found in chalk deposits in western Kansas.

THE DINOSAUR RE-EVOLVED?

A number of huge, flightless, hunting birds evolved around 65 million years ago, once the dinosaurs died out. *Phorusrhachos* of South America and *Diatryma* of North America were built along the lines of medium-sized meat-eating dinosaurs, with fast hind legs and fierce heads. *Titanis* (above) from Florida even had tiny clawed hands on the remains of its wings — almost as if a niche developed for dinosaur-shaped hunting creatures and evolution filled it with giant hunting birds.

KILLER DUCK

Bullockornis lived in Australia around 20 million years ago. It stood 10 feet (3 m) high and had a huge beak that was used for either cracking nuts or tearing flesh. An enlarged brain capacity suggests that the latter was more likely, since quick senses are necessary for hunting prey. *Bullockornis* was unrelated to the emus or the cassowaries or to any other type of flightless bird that exists in Australia today. Despite its dinosaur-like appearance, *Bullockornis* was actually a kind of duck.

ABANDONING FLIGHT

It seems to some scientists that often no sooner has a feature evolved than certain lines of evolution abandon it. As soon as flight evolved, some birds reverted to living on the ground. There are several explanations for this. Perhaps flightless birds evolved in areas where no dangerous predators lived on the ground, and so there was no need to fly, or perhaps food was more plentiful on the ground.

DEAD AS A DODO

Probably the best known of the extinct, flightless birds is *Raphus*, the dodo. The dodo evolved from pigeon stock into a ground-dwelling plant eater on the island of Mauritius. It survived there for thousands of years, as there were no ground-living predators. Everything changed, however, when humans arrived on the island, and the bird was wiped out within a few years.

PLANT EATERS

Not only were the shapes of the meat-eating dinosaurs reflected in some of the later birds, but bird versions of the long-necked plant eaters seem to have existed as well. *Dinorinis*, the moa, existed in New Zealand up to modern times. It thrived there because no ground-living predators lived in New Zealand — until human beings came along and wiped out the bird.

LATE CRETACEOUS 97-65 MYA	PALEOGENE 65-23 MYA	NEOGENE 23-1.8 MYA	QUATERNARY 1.8-0.01 MYA

SINCE THE DINOSAURS

The end of the Cretaceous Period was marked by a mass extinction. The birds were a bit luckier than other creatures. They lost three-quarters of their species, but the remaining one-quarter soon re-established themselves as the masters of the skies. As the mammals spread in the absence of dinosaurs, they also took to the skies. The bats developed successfully, and other mammal groups developed gliding forms. There were even gliding reptiles and amphibians. Throughout all this, insects continued to buzz, as they have done since Carboniferous times.

THE WEBBED WAY

The birds that survived the mass extinction went on to become the true masters of the skies. Birds today mostly fly, but they can also perch, wade, swim, and even burrow. *Presbyornis* was a long-legged wading duck that lived in huge flocks in North America around 65 million years ago. Although it had webbed feet, its legs would have been too long to allow it to swim. The webs probably developed to prevent it from sinking into the mud.

THE TRUE KINGS

Insects appeared nearly 400 million years ago and immediately evolved flying types. Few died out in the mass extinction at the end of the Cretaceous, and they are now far more diverse than any other group of creatures. Wings are the tough parts of an insect's anatomy, and it is mostly wings that have been fossilized. Occasionally the preservation is so good that the patterns and markings are preserved, although the colors have long since changed.

LATE CRETACEOUS 97-65 MYA	PALEOGENE 65-23 MYA	NEOGENE 23-1.8 MYA	QUATERNARY 1.8-0.01 MYA

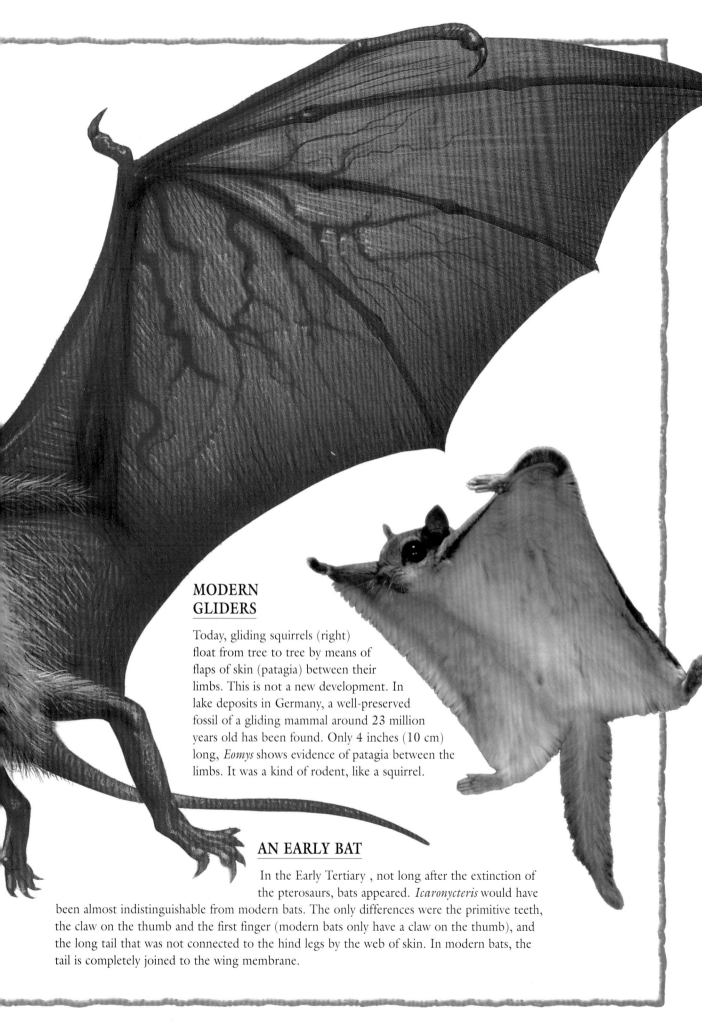

MODERN GLIDERS

Today, gliding squirrels (right) float from tree to tree by means of flaps of skin (patagia) between their limbs. This is not a new development. In lake deposits in Germany, a well-preserved fossil of a gliding mammal around 23 million years old has been found. Only 4 inches (10 cm) long, *Eomys* shows evidence of patagia between the limbs. It was a kind of rodent, like a squirrel.

AN EARLY BAT

In the Early Tertiary , not long after the extinction of the pterosaurs, bats appeared. *Icaronycteris* would have been almost indistinguishable from modern bats. The only differences were the primitive teeth, the claw on the thumb and the first finger (modern bats only have a claw on the thumb), and the long tail that was not connected to the hind legs by the web of skin. In modern bats, the tail is completely joined to the wing membrane.

DID YOU KNOW?

• It is very unusual for a dinosaur to form a fossil. Fossils are nearly always of water-living animals. The rocks in which we find fossils are formed of sediment built up on the bottom of seas, lakes, rivers, and sometimes deserts. When a land animal dies, it is eaten by meat-eating scavengers that pull the skeleton to pieces. Any leftover pieces are nibbled away by insects or rotted by bacteria. For a dinosaur to become a fossil, its body would have to fall into water and be immediately buried in sediment where nothing could reach it.

• We only know of about a fifth of the dinosaur species that ever lived. It would be very difficult for a dinosaur living in an upland forest or on a mountain slope ever to become fossilized. Looking at the variety of animals today and their wide range of habitats, scientists estimate that probably between 1,200 and 1,500 different dinosaur species existed. We know of about 300.

• We do not know whether any dinosaur climbed trees. Tree-living animals do not tend to become fossils. The trees are often a long way from the ocean or anywhere that fossils may form. Also, tree-living animals are lightweight, with delicate skeletons that tend to break easily. But some scientists think that maniraptorans developed their curved claws to climb tree trunks and hang on to branches. Some scientists even think that the huge claws of *Deinocheirus* were needed by a gigantic slothlike climbing dinosaur. These ideas are all just scientific theories, however.

• Dinosaurs are given long, scientific names that are usually based on Latin or ancient Greek words. Scientists all over the world can then understand the names, no matter what language they usually speak.

• Scientific names for dinosaurs have two parts, like Tyrannosaurus rex. The first part of any plant or animal's scientific name is its genus name, and the second part is the species name. Usually, when the name is not used in a scientific setting, only the genus name is used. Scientific names are always printed in italics. The genus part always has a capital letter, but the species part does not. These rules hold even if the name is based on the name of a person or a place.

• Water animals adjust their buoyancy in different ways. Deep divers, such as whales, ichthyosaurs, and seals, have heavy bodies and small lungs. In contrast, animals that walk on the seabed, such as placodonts, desmostylans, and dugongs, have heavy bones and large lungs. Animals that "fly" underwater, such as sea lions, plesiosaurs, and penguins, swallow stones to adust their buoyancy.

• Some sea animals in existence today are bigger than any sea animals of the past. At 93 feet (28 m), the blue whale is much larger than any extinct sea animal known.

• There are two kinds of flight in the animal kingdom – flapping flight and gliding flight. Flapping flight requires the animal to provide all the muscular energy to produce the flying action. Gliding flight simply requires the animal to have a certain shape of wing to soar through the air. Flapping flight is seen in birds and in pterosaurs. This kind of flight may lapse into gliding flight, when, for example, a vulture soars on rising hot air, looking for food.

• There are two types of gliding flight. In one type, the gliding action is initiated by the animal's own muscular efforts. Flying fish, for example, launch themselves into the air by swimming rapidly to the surface and using the movement of their strong tails to throw themselves out of the water. In the second type of gliding flight, the animal simply drops down from a high vantage point and uses its aerodynamic shape to take it where it wants to go. Flying squirrels and the flying dragon lizards of Malaysia do this type of gliding to take them from a higher place to a lower place.

• Scientists disagree as to how bird flight evolved. Some say that primitive birds, such as Archaeopteryx, started as gliders. Others see these birds as essentially terrestrial creatures, launching themselves into the air by running quickly along the ground.

GLOSSARY

alula - a tuft of feathers on a bird's wing that helps the bird maintain control while in flight by influencing how air moves over the wing.

ammonites - extinct, mollusk-like marine animals of the Mesozoic age that had flat, spiral shells.

anatomy - the structure of a body or of an organ. Anatomists study anatomy.

articulated – joined at a certain angle at a joint, often used in explaining how an animal moves.

aquatic - living or growing in or near water.

ballast - weight that produces stability and control.

bivalve - a mollusk, such as an oyster or a clam, that has a shell made of two parts, or valves, joined with a flexible elastic hinge.

buoyancy - the tendency to float or rise when submerged in a liquid.

carrion - dead and decaying flesh.

chitin - the organic substance that forms the hard outer shell of insects, arachnids and crustaceans.

crests - a projection, such as a tuft of feathers or fur, on the head of a bird or some other kind of animal.

DNA - an acid inside every living cell that carries genetic information about individual heredity.

drought - a long, dry period of low rainfall.

evolved - changed and developed over long periods of time so that descendants look or behave differently than their early ancestors.

expedition - a journey with a specific goal.

extinct - no longer existing or living.

food chain - a feeding cycle in which each plant or animal becomes food for another, and so on.

flanges - ridges or collarlike projections on the edges of some objects that add strength and to which other objects can be attached.

fossil - remnants or impressions of organisms from a past geologic age embedded in natural materials such as rock or resin.

gastroliths - stones that an animal swallows to help its digestion by grinding food.

genus - a grouping of related plants or animals. A family is the most broad grouping, a genus is next, and a species is the most specific grouping.

gullet - the throat or food tube area.

invertebrate - a living organism that does not have a backbone.

mammals - warm-blooded, vertebrate animals, including human beings, that have hair or fur on their skin and nourish their young with milk produced in the mammary glands of the female's body.

membrane - a thin, pliable layer of tissue that covers or separates certain parts of an animal's body, such as its organs.

metabolic - related to the processes within living organisms by which chemical changes convert food into energy.

migrate - to move to another land area because of a season or climate change.

natural selection - a theory that only the plants or animals that have the best characteristics to survive in a certain environment will live and reproduce.

plate tectonics - the theory that Earth's continents were once a single landmass that drifted or were forced apart over billions of years.

paleontologist - a scientist who studies fossils to learn about past ages.

Pangaea - the single mass of land that existed on Earth in prehistoric times, before the continents drifted apart.

plates - smooth, flat, relatively thin bonelike structures, usually growing on the back, that helped protect herbivores.

plumage - the feathers of a bird.

predator - an animal that hunts other animals for food.

prey - an animal that is hunted by another animal for food.

pygostyle - the muscular, stumplike tailbone of some birds, which contains vertebrae that are fused, or joined, and which controls the movement of tail feathers.

quarries - large, open pits or excavations of land that are dug out to obtain stone, sand, or gravel.

ranged - could be found in certain areas.

raptor - a bird of prey, such as a hawk.

reptiles - cold-blooded vertebrates such as snakes, turtles, or crocodiles, that lay eggs and have horny plates or scales.

scavenger - an animal that feeds on dead or decaying matter.

sediment (silt) - mud and other fine materials that settle at the bottom of water.

serrated - having a toothed, notched, cutting edge.

sheath - in animals, a protective tube that surrounds a body part.

spawning - when fish lay their eggs.

species - a group of plants or animals that are very alike. A species is the most narrow, specific scientific grouping.

sponges - primitive marine animals with porous skeletons that grow like plants and attach to surfaces underwater.

struts - bars or rods used to brace a structure against pressure along its length.

taphonomy - the study of the processes by which organisms become fossils.

tendon - a band of tough, fibrous tissue that connects a muscle to a bone.

vertebrae - a living organism that has a backbone or spinal column.

INDEX

A

Acheluosaurus 65
Albertosaurus 30
Alioramus 30, 31
alligators 14
Allosaurus 18, 21, 32
Allosaurus atrox 31
alula 118
alvarezsaurids 24, 25
Alvarezsaurus 25
amber 97
ammonites 90
Ampelosaurus 45
amphibians 122
Anchisaurus 38
ankylosaurids 55-6, 58-9
Anning, Mary 84, 105
Antarctica 12
anteater 28
Anurognathus 113
Apatosaurus (formerly *Brontosaurus*) 42
Appalachian Mountains 10
Arambourgiania 113
Archaeoceratops 63
Archaeopteryx 21, 24, 114-15, 119, 124
Archelon 70
Argentavis 112
Argentinosaurus 44
armor 44-5, 52-3, 55-7
  nodosaurids 56, 57
  sauropods 44, 45
  stegosaurids 52, 53, 55

B

Bambiraptor 21, 116
Baptanodon 71
Baryonyx 14
Basilosaurus 71

bats 101, 103, 105-6, 122-3
beaks 28, 51, 63, 108, 111, 118
Beipiaosaurus 29
belemnites 89
Bernissart, Belgium 48
birds 11-12, 21, 24-5, 96-7, 106, 120-2
bones 28, 41, 44, 112
  hip 46, 54, 58
  neck 40
  see also jaws; skulls
Brachiosaurus 42, 43
Brontosaurus (now *Apatosaurus*) 42
Buckland, Revd William 8, 9
buoyancy 69, 72, 124

C

Caenagnathus 22
Camarasaurus 19
Carcharodontosaurus 32, 33
Caudipteryx 116
ceratopsians 62-5
Ceratosaurus 13
Ceresiosaurus 74
champosaurs 92
Changchengornis 119
Chasmosaurus 64
China, Liaoning 13, 117-19
Chirostenotes 22
claws 19-20
Coelophysis 10-11
Coelurosauravus 96, 98
coelurosaurids 16
Compsognathus 17, 114
Confuciusornis 118-19
conifers 51, 116
Connecticut 10, 11

convergent evolution 73
Conybeare, William 91
coprolite 31
crests 12-13, 26, 110, 111
crocodiles 14, 71, 77, 92-3
Cryolophosaurus 12
Cryptoclidus 81
Crystal Palace, London 8, 48, 100
Cuvier, Baron Georges 90-1, 101
cycads 63, 116
Cymbospondylus 71, 86

D

Dacenturus 55
Darwin, Charles 108, 114
Daspletosaurus 30, 31
De la Beche, Sir Henry 101
defense 41, 64, 73
  see also armor
Deinocheirus 26, 124
Deinonychus 20-1, 116
Deinosuchus 93
Delphinosaurus 71
Diatryma 120
Dicracosaurus 55
Dilophosaurus 12-13
Dimorphodon 104
Dinorinis (moa) 121
Diplodocus 37, 40-1, 43, 55
dodo 121
Dolichorhynchops 71, 79
Dorset, England 76, 84
dromaeosaurids 20-2
Dsungaripterus 111
duckbills 50-1, 74

E

eggs 22-3, 83
Einiosaurus 65
elasmosaurs 76-8, 80-3
Elasmosaurus 82
emu 27
Eoalulavis 118
Eomys 123
Eoraptor 6-7
Erlikosaurus 28
Eudimorphodon 102-3
Euoplocephalus 58
Eurhinosaurus 86-7
Euskelosaurus 38
Eustreptospondylus 8
evolution 73, 83, 92, 108

F

feathers 23, 29, 106, 114, 117
feet 11, 16, 18, 28, 45, 63, 119, 122
  Allosaurus 18
  ceratopsians 63
  Changchengornis 119
  Erlikosaurus 28
  ornithopods 46
  sauropods 46
  webbed 122
flight 99, 103, 118, 122-4
flying reptiles 97, 98, 99
food 10, 15, 31
  ankylosaurids 59
  birds 121
  hadrosaurs 51
  Iguanodon 49
  placodonts 72
  pterodactyloids 108
  sauropods 51
fossils 9, 11, 16, 70, 124

INDEX

fur 100, 102, 106-7, 117

G

Gallimimus 26
Garidumimus 26
Gasparinisaura 49
Gastonia 56
gastroliths (stomach stones) 40, 76
Geosaurus 92
gharials 92, 93
Gigantosaurus 32, 33
Globidens 91
Gobi Desert 23, 24

H

hadrosaurs 46, 50, 51
Hadrosaurus 51
Hawkins, Thomas 100
heads 9, 64, 110-11
heat regulation 48, 52, 65
Henodus 73
Herrerasaurus 6
Hesperornis 120
Heterodontosaurus 47
Holzmaden, Germany 84, 88-9, 93
Homalocephale 60
horns 12, 60-1, 64-5
Hovasaurus 69
Huayangosaurus 55
Hydrotherosaurus 83
Hylaeosaurus 9
Hypsilophodon 46, 47

I

Iberomesornis 119
Icaronycteris 123
Icarosaurus 99
ichthyosaurs 71, 80, 84-9
iguanas 69
Iguanodon 9, 46, 48-9, 51

iguanodontids 48-50
insects 97, 122
intestines, ornithopods 46, 47
Irritator 14, 15

I

jaws 14, 46
Jurassic Park (film) 97

K

Kansas 112, 113
Kazakhstan 107
Kentrosaurus 54
Kronosaurus 78
Kuelmeosaurus 98

L

Lariosaurus 74
Liaoning, China 13, 117-19
Liopleurodon 78
Loch Ness monster 80
Longisquama 99
Lufengosaurus 39

M

mammals 6, 122
maniraptorans 20, 22, 24-5, 116, 124
Mantell, Gideon and Mary 48
Martin, John 100
Megalosaurus 8-9, 48
Meganeura 97
Megaraptor 21
Melanorosaurus 39
Mesosaurus 68
Metriorhynchus 71, 92
Micropachycephalosaurus 61
Mixosaurus 86
moa 121
Monolophosaurus 13
Mononykus 24-5

monophyletic evolution 83
Montanoceratops 63
Morocco 32
Morrison Formation 18-19, 42-4
mosasaurs 71, 85, 90-1
Mosasaurus 71
Moschops 6
muscles 18
Mussaurus 36
Muttaburrasaurus 48, 49

N

names, scientific 31, 124
Nanotyrannus 30, 31
Navajopus 39
necks 40, 81-3
nests 22-3
New Mexico 11, 30
Newman, Edward 100
nodosaurids 55-7, 59
nothosaurs 74-5, 83
Nothosaurus 74
Nqwebasaurus 16

O

One Million Years BC (film) 102
Ophthalmosaurus 86
The Origin of Species (Darwin) 114
ornithomimids 26-7
ornithopods 46-7, 50
ostriches 24, 26-7
Ouranosaurus 48 22-3
Owen, Sir Richard 9

P

pachycephalosaurids 60-1
Pachycephalosaurus 61
pachystosis 72, 76

Pangaea 11, 37, 39, 42, 68
Patagonykus 25
Pelecanimimys 26
Phorusrhachos 120
phytosaurs 92
Placochelys 73
placodonts 72-3
plants 59, 63
plate tectonics 68
Plateosaurus 36-7
platypus, duckbilled 74
plesiosaurs 71, 75, 86
Plioplatecarpus 91
pliosaurs 76-81, 83
Plocodus 72
Plotosaurus 91
polyphyletic theory 83
Prenocephale 60
Presbyornis 122
Proganochelys 70
prosauropods 28, 36-9, 46
Protoarchaeopteryx 117
Protoceratops 23, 62
Psephoderma 73
Psittacosaurus 63
Pteranodon 110, 112-13
pterodactyloids 103-4, 108-9
Pterodactylus 108, 109
pterosaurs 96-7, 100-7
pygostyles 118-19

Q

Quetzalcoatlus 112

R

Rahonavis 20
Raphus (dodo) 121
raptors 20-1
rauisuchians 7
reptiles 6-9, 36, 71, 122

INDEX

rhamphorhynchoids
    103-5, 109, 113
rhea 25
Rhomaleosaurus 79
rhynchosaurs 36
Riojasaurus 38-9
Rocky Mountains 11

S

Sahara 14
Saltasaurus 45
Sauropelta 57
sauropods 40-6, 50-1
Sauroposeidon 43
Scelidosaurus 55
Scipionyx 16
segnosaurids 28-9
Segnosaurus 29
Seismosaurus 43
Seisomosaurus 37
sharks 82
Sharovipteryx 98
sheep 60, 62
Shonisaurus 86
Shunosaurus 41
Sinornis 96
Sinosauropteryx 117
skulls 7, 18, 46, 61, 77
Sordes 107

speed 26-7
Spinoaequalis 68
Spinosaurids 14-15
Spinosaurus 14-15, 48
Stegoceras 60-1
stegosaurids 54-5
Stegosaurus 52-4
Steneosaurus 93
stomach stones
    (gastroliths) 40, 69,
    76
Struthiomimus 26-7
Struthiosaurus 57
Stygimoloch 60
Styracosaurus 64
Suchomimus 14
swimming 80, 82,
    86-7, 120
Syntarsus 11

T

tails 41, 51, 54, 58, 68,
    119
Tanzania 13
Tapejara 110
taphonomy 52, 70
teeth
    elasmosaurs 83
    herbivores and

carnivores 36
Iguanodon 48
Mesosaurus 68
nothosaurs 75
ornithomimids 26
ornithopods 46, 47
placodonts 73
pterosaurs 103
sauropods 43
Teleosaurus 92
Tenontosaurus 20, 48-9
Tethys Ocean 72, 75
Thamphorbynchus 106
Thecodontosaurus 38, 39
therizinosaurids 28-9
Therizinosaurus 29
theropods 6
Titanis 120
titanosaurids 45
Triceratops 31, 65
Troodon 22-3
Tropeognathus 110
Tupuxuara 110
turtles 70, 81
Tylosaurus 91
tyrannosaurids 30-1
Tyrannosaurus 15,
    30-3, 36, 58

U

Unenlagia 25
Utahraptor 21, 116

V

Velociraptor 21, 116
Velociraptor
    mongoliensis 31

W

Wagler, Johann 100
walrus 73
whales 71
wings 24-5, 98
    Archaeopteryx 115
    Eoalulavis 118
    insects 122
    pterosaurs 102-3,
        106-7
wingspan, pterosaurs
    112
Wuerhosaurus 55

Y

young, ichthyosaurs
    88, 89

Z

Zimbabwe 11
Zygorbiza 71

ACKNOWLEDGMENTS

The original publisher would like to thank Advocate and Elizabeth Wiggans for their assistance.

Picture Credits: t=top, b=bottom, c=center, l=left, r=right

Lisa Alderson: 6bl, 6/7c, 16/17c, 24l, 25c, 29c, 33b, 43cr, 46b, 47b, 48b, 58-59c, 60-61c. 69b, 70-71c, 79t, 80-81c, 86-87, 92c. 98b, 105b, 106-107c, 112cl, 116b, 117b, 121bl. John Alston: 6tl, 10/11c, 11t, 16t, 16b, 18tl, 19t, 22cl, 22bl, 25tr, 28tl, 28bl, 29tr, 30tl, 36tr, 36b, 37t, 41cr, 42t, 50b, 52t, 53c, 57tr, 58b, 63t, 64t. 68b, 70l, 71r, 72b, 73r, 75t, 80t, 82l, 83t, 87t, 88cl, 88b, 90t. 103b, 107t. Australian Museum: 40tl, 76tr. A-Z Botanical: 49b, 51tr, 59cr. BBC Natural History Unit: 60b, 64b. 69tr, 73t, 74tl, 77cr, 90c, 93b. 106cl, 123b. Dr. Jose Bonaparte: 36t. Corbis: 10tl, 13b, 24b, 25tr, 27tr, 27br, 28cb. 75b, 90bl. 106b, 108cr. Dougal Dixon: 7b, 8b, 12b, 13tl, 13tr, 21b, 33tr, 79b.Steve Etches: 76cl. Fossil Finds: 6cl, 16c, 23tr, 31br, 39t, 45t, 62cl, 63b. 70b, 84t, 90cl.Dr Peter Griffith: 17t, 21c, 114t, 114b, 115cr. Humboldt Museum: 42cl, 55t. Kobal Collection: 102t. Simon Mendez: 10/11b, 12-13c, 14-15c, 18/19c, 19b, 20b, 20/21c, 22t, 26/27c, 31cr, 32c, 36-37c, 38t, 38-39c, 40-41c, 42-43b, 44b, 48-49c, 52-53c, 54-55c, 56-57c, 60t, 64-65c, 68c, 72-73c, 74-75c, 78-79c, 83cr, 83br, 89c & OFC, 90-91c, 92bl. 96-97, 98-99c, 104c, 105t, 108c, 110t, 117b, 118t, 119t, 119b, 120c, 122cl. Museum of Utah: 56tl.National Trust: 41cl. National Museum of Wales: 101c, 111t. Natural History Museum: 11cr, 14tl, 31t. 46t, 46cl, 47t, 48ct, 51t, 52b, 55cr, 56b, 58cl, 61b, 61tr, 63cr, 64cl, 78tl, 81tr, 86b, 89t, 90b, 100c, 102b, 104t, 108t, 113cr, 121t. Bob Nicholls: 76-77c. Oxford City Museum: 8tl, 8c, 9tr. Paleontologisk museum, Oslo: 98cl, 99cr, 118c. Peterborough Museum: 77b. Planet Earth Pictures: 14bl. Luis Rey: 23c, 30/31c. 44t, 45c, 50-51c, 62-63c, 72t, 82-83c, 84-85c, 92-93c. 99b, 102-103c, 109c, 111c, 112-113c, 115b, 116t, 117tr, 120cl, 122-123c. Royal Tyrell Museum: 87cr. Science Photo Library: 80b. Paul Sereno: 7cr, 32tr. Professor Kent Stephens: p41t. University of Bristol: 85b. University of Toronto: 68tr.